BRIEF CONTENTS

Windows Server 2008 Applications Infrastructure Configuration

Lab Manual

WILEY

EXECUTIVE EDITOR	John Kane
EDITORIAL ASSISTANT	Jennifer Lartz
DIRECTOR OF MARKETING AND SALES	Mitchell Beaton
PRODUCTION MANAGER	Micheline Frederick
PRODUCTION EDITOR	Kerry Weinstein
DEVELOPMENT AND PRODUCTION	Custom Editorial Productions, Inc.

To order books or for customer service, please call 1-800-CALL WILEY (225-5945).

ISBN   978-0-470-22512-7

Printed in the United States of America

10 9 8 7 6 5 4

CONTENTS

Windows Server 2008 Applications Infrastructure Configuration

Lab Manual

LAB 1
PREPARING AN APPLICATION SERVER

This lab contains the following exercises and activities:

Exercise 1.1	Performing Initial Configuration Tasks
Exercise 1.2	Working with Disks
Exercise 1.3	Using Server Manager
Exercise 1.4	Adding the File Services Role
Lab Review	Questions
Lab Challenge	Using Diskpart.exe

BEFORE YOU BEGIN

The classroom network consists of Windows Server 2008 student servers and the ServerDC connected to a local area network. ServerDC, the domain controller for the contoso.com domain, is running Windows Server 2008. Throughout the labs in this manual, you will install, configure, maintain, and troubleshoot application roles, features, and services on the same student server.

Before you start this lab, see your instructor for the information needed to complete the following table:

Student computer name (Server##)	
Student account name (Student##)	

Working with Lab Worksheets

Each lab in this manual requires that you answer questions, save images of your screen, or perform other activities that you document in a worksheet named for the lab, such as *lab01_worksheet*. Your instructor placed the worksheet files in the Students\Worksheets share on ServerDC. As you perform the exercises in each lab, open the appropriate worksheet file using WordPad, fill in the required information, and save the file to your computer's Student##\Documents folder. This folder is automatically redirected to the ServerDC computer. Your instructor will examine these worksheet files to assess your performance.

The procedure for opening and saving a worksheet file is as follows:

1.   Click Start, and then click Run. The Run dialog box appears.

2.   In the Open text box, key **ServerDC\Students\Worksheets\lab##_worksheet** (where lab## contains the number of the lab you're completing), and click OK. The worksheet document opens in WordPad.

3.   Complete all of the exercises in the worksheet.

4.   In WordPad, choose Save As from the File menu. The Save As dialog box appears.

5.   In the File Name text box, key **lab##_worksheet_*yourname*** (where lab## contains the number of the lab you're completing, and *yourname* is your last name), and click Save.

SCENARIO

You are a new administrator for Contoso, Ltd., working on a test deployment of the application server technologies included with Windows Server 2008. In this lab, you prepare a new computer for deployment as a file server.

After completing this lab, you will be able to:

- ■ Perform initial configuration tasks
- ■ Prepare hard disk drives for deployment
- ■ Use the Server Manager console
- ■ Install the File Services role

Estimated lab time: 70 minutes

Exercise 1.1	Performing Initial Configuration Tasks
Overview	You are setting up a new computer that was delivered with Windows Server 2008 already installed in its default configuration. Your first task is to configure the computer with appropriate settings for the test lab network.
Completion time	10 minutes

1. Turn on your computer. When the logon screen appears, log on using the local Administrator account and the password *P@ssw0rd*. The Initial Configuration Tasks window appears, as shown in Figure 1-1.

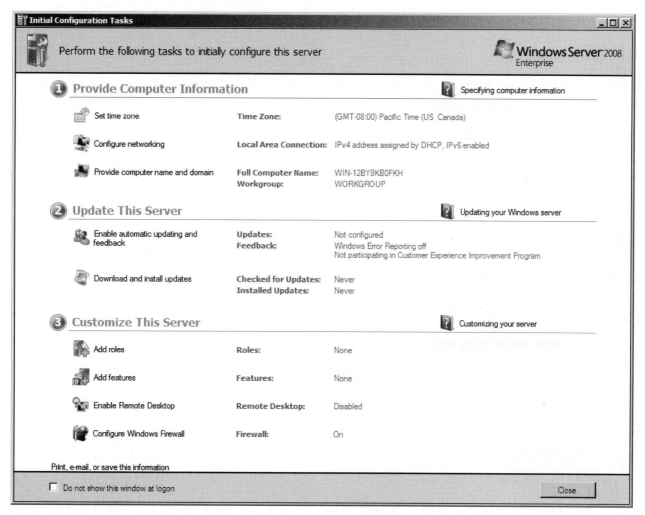

Figure 1-1
Initial Configuration Tasks window

2.   Click Set Time Zone. The Date And Time dialog box appears.

3.   Make sure that the date, time, and time zone shown in the dialog box are correct. If they are not, click Change Date And Time or Change Time Zone and correct them. Then, click OK.

4.   Click Provide Computer Name And Domain. The System Properties dialog box appears with the Computer Name tab selected.

5.   Click Change. The Computer Name/Domain Changes dialog box appears.

6.   In the Computer Name text box, key **Server##**, where ##, supplied by your instructor, identifies your computer.

7.   Select the Domain option key **contoso.com** in the text box, and click OK. A Windows Security dialog box appears.

8.   In the User Name test box, key **Administrator**. Key **P@ssw0rd** in the Password text box, and click OK. A message box appears, welcoming you to the contoso.com domain.

Question 1	Which computer is hosting the Administrator account that you specified in this authentication?

9.   Click OK. A message box appears, prompting you to restart your computer.

10.   Click OK, and then click Close to close the System Properties dialog box. Another message box appears, informing you again that you must restart the computer.

11.   Click Restart Now. The computer restarts.

12.   Log on to the domain with your *Student##* account, where ## is the number assigned by your instructor, using the password *P@ssw0rd*.

13.   Press Ctrl+Prt Scr to take a screen shot of the Initial Configuration Tasks window, and then press Ctrl+V to paste the image on the page provided in the lab01_worksheet file.

14.   Leave the computer logged on for the next exercise.

NOTE	*Completing the initial configuration tasks in this exercise leaves the student computer in its baseline state, which is the computer's expected configuration at the beginning of each subsequent lab. If your class uses virtual machines, you might have to repeat the steps of this exercise before you begin each lab.*

Exercise 1.2	Working with Disks
Overview	The new computer arrived with two installed disk drives, but only the first one is initialized and partitioned. In this exercise, you will initialize the second disk and create data partitions on the computer.
Completion time	20 minutes

1. Click Start, and then click Administrative Tools > Computer Management. A User Account Control dialog box appears, prompting you for your permission to continue.

2. Click Continue. The Computer Management console appears.

3. In the Computer Management console's scope (left) pane, select Disk Management. The Disk Management snap-in appears in the details (right) pane, as shown in Figure 1-2.

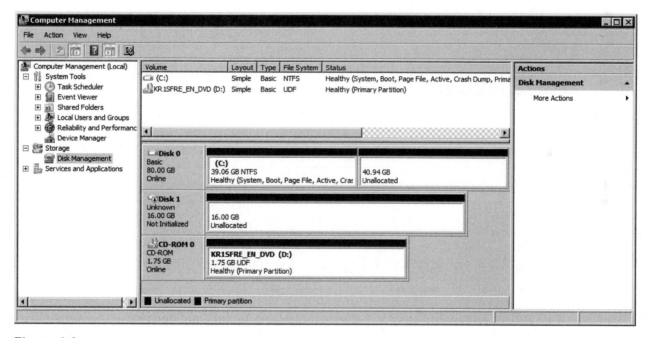

Figure 1-2
Disk Management snap-in

4. Immediately after the snap-in appears, an Initialize Disk dialog box appears, prompting you to select a partition style for Disk 1. Leave the default MBR (Master Boot Record) option selected, and click OK.

Question 2	*Why is the system prompting you to initialize Disk 1 at this time?*
Question 3	*What happens to the Disk 1 type and status when the initialization process is complete?*
Question 4	*Now that Disk 1 has been initialized, why doesn't it appear in the volume list pane at the top of the console?*

5. Based on the information displayed in the Disk Management snap-in, fill out the information in Table 1-1 on your lab worksheet.

Table 1-1
Disk information

	Disk 0	Disk 1
Disk type (basic or dynamic)		
Total disk size		
Number and type of partitions		
Amount of unallocated space		

NOTE	*If at least one gigabyte of unallocated space is not available on your workstation's Disk 0, see your instructor before you continue.*

6. In the graphical display, right-click the Unallocated area of Disk 0 and, from the context menu, select New Simple Volume. The New Simple Volume Wizard appears.

7. Click Next to bypass the *Welcome* page. The *Specify Volume Size* page appears.

8. In the Simple Volume Size In MB text box, key **5000** and click Next. The *Assign Drive Letter Or Path* page appears.

9. Leave the Assign The Following Drive Letter radio button selected, select drive letter X from the drop-down list, and click Next. The *Format Partition* page appears.

10. Leave the Format This Partition With The Following Settings radio button selected, and configure the next three parameters as follows:

    - File System: NTFS

    - Allocation Unit Size: Default

    - Volume Label: Data1

11. Select the Perform A Quick Format checkbox and click Next. The *Completing The New Simple Volume Wizard* page appears.

12. Click Finish. The new Data1 volume appears in the console.

13. Using the same procedure, create another simple volume using the rest of the unallocated space on Disk 0, assigning it the drive letter Y and the volume name Data2.

14. Right-click the Data2 volume you created. A context menu appears.

Question 5	What volume sizing options are available in the context menu?
Question 6	Why are you unable to extend the Data2 volume to Disk 1?

15. Right-click Disk 0 and, from the context menu, select Convert To Dynamic Disk. The Convert To Dynamic Disk dialog box appears.

16. Click OK. The Disks To Convert dialog box appears.

17. Click Convert. A Disk Management message box appears containing a warning about boot limitations from dynamic disks.

18. Click Yes. Disk 0 changes from a basic to a dynamic disk.

19. Right-click the Data2 volume and, from the context menu, select Extend Volume. The Extend Volume Wizard appears.

20. Click Next to bypass the *Welcome* page. The *Select Disks* page appears.

21. Select Disk 1 in the Available box, and click Add. Disk 1 moves to the Selected box.

22. Using the Select The Amount Of Space In MB spin box, allocate approximately half of the available space on Disk 1 to the Data2 volume.

23. Click Next. The *Completing The Extend Volume Wizard* page appears.

24. Click Finish. A Disk Management message box appears, informing you that the process of extending the volume will cause the selected basic disk to be converted to a dynamic disk.

Question 7	*Why is it necessary to convert both of the disks?*

25. Click Yes. The Data2 volume is extended to include half of the available space on Disk 1.

26. Repeat the procedure to extend the volume in Disk 0 containing the C: drive to the remaining space on Disk 1.

Question 8	*Why are you unable to extend the C: drive to Disk 1?*

27. Consult the Disk Management snap-in, and fill out Table 1-2 with the amount of unallocated space on the drive in gigabytes and megabytes.

Table 1-2
Unallocated space remaining

	Disk 0	Disk 1
Unallocated space left (in gigabytes)		
Unallocated space left (in megabytes)		

28. Press Ctrl+Prt Scr to take a screen shot of the Disk Management snap-in showing the volumes you created. Press Ctrl+V to paste the image on the page provided in the lab01_worksheet file.

29. Close the Computer Management console, and leave the computer logged on for the next exercise.

Exercise 1.3	Using Server Manager
Overview	In the future, you will need to configure your server to perform certain tasks, using tools and services that Windows Server 2008 does not install by default. In this exercise, use the Server Manager console to configure the server and install these tools and services.
Completion time	10 minutes

1. Click Start, point to Administrative Tools, and click Server Manager. Click Continue in the User Account Control message box. The Server Manager console appears, as shown in Figure 1-3.

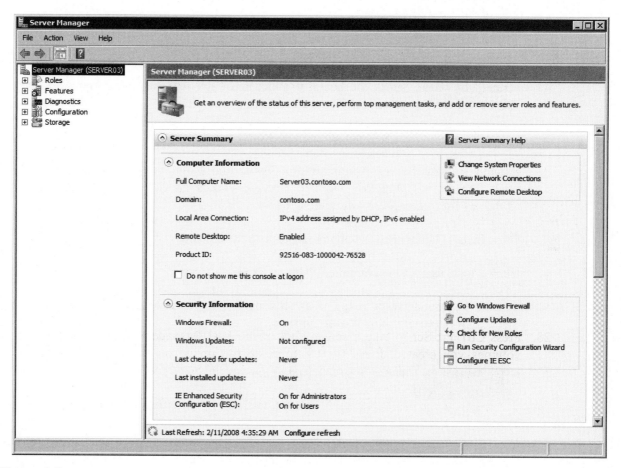

Figure 1-3
Server Manager console

Question 9	Which of the previous tasks could be completed using Server Manager instead of other consoles?

2. In the Server Summary section under Security Information, click Configure IE ESC. The Internet Explorer Enhanced Security Configuration dialog box appears.

3. Under Administrators, select the Off option, and click OK.

Question 10	Based on the information in the main Server Manager display, what roles are currently installed on the computer?
Question 11	What features are currently installed on the computer?

4. In the scope pane, select the Features node, and click Add Features. The Add Features Wizard appears, displaying the *Select Features* page.

5. Select the Group Policy Management checkbox.

6. Expand Remote Server Administration Tools and Role Administration Tools. Then, select the Active Directory Domain Services Tools checkbox, and click Next. The *Confirm Installation Selections* page appears.

7. Click Install. The wizard installs the features you selected.

8. Click Close. Restart the computer when prompted.

9. When the computer restarts, log on as Student##. The Server Manager console opens, and the Resume Configuration Wizard appears.

Question 12	What was the result of the installation?

10. Press Ctrl+Prt Scr to take a screen shot of the *Installation Results* page in the Resume Configuration Wizard. Press Ctrl+V to paste the image on the page provided in the lab01_worksheet file.

11. Click Close.

12. Leave Server Manager open for the next exercise.

Exercise 1.4	Adding the File Services Role
Overview	Install the File Services role by using the Server Manager console. This enables you to deploy this computer as a file server and implement the various storage-related technologies supplied with Windows Server 2008.
Completion time	10 minutes

1. In the Server Manager scope pane, select the Roles node, and then click Add Roles. The Add Roles Wizard appears, displaying the *Before You Begin* page.

2. Click Next. The *Select Server Roles* page appears, as shown in Figure 1-4.

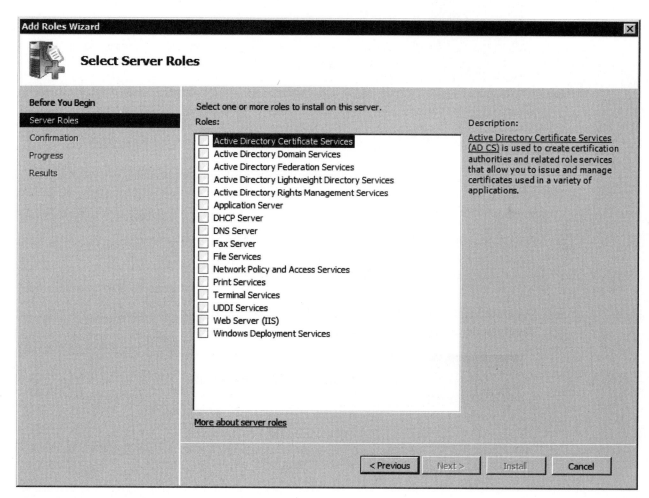

Figure 1-4
Select Server Roles page of the Add Roles Wizard

3. Select the File Services checkbox, and click Next.

Question 13	What happens to the wizard when you select the File Services checkbox?

4. Click Next to bypass the *Introduction To File Services* page. The *Select Role Services* page appears.

5. Select the Services For Network File System and Windows Search Service role service checkboxes.

Question 14	What happens to the wizard when you select the Windows Search Services checkbox?
Question 15	What happens to the wizard if you select the Windows Server 2003 File Services checkbox?

6. Click Next to continue. The *Volumes To Index* page appears.

7. Select the Local Disk (C:) checkbox, and click Next. The *Confirmation* page appears.

8. Click Install. The wizard installs the role and the selected role services.

9. Click Close to close the wizard.

10. Press Ctrl+Prt Scr to take a screen shot of the Roles node in server manager, showing the details for the installed File Services role. Press Ctrl+V to paste the image on the page provided in the lab01_worksheet file.

11. Close Server Manager, and log off of the computer.

LAB REVIEW: QUESTIONS

Completion time	5 minutes

1. After creating a spanned volume containing space from two disks, as you did in Exercise 1.2, what happens to the data stored on the volume if Disk 1 fails?

2. In Exercise 1.2, how many partitions does each disk have after you converted the disks from basic to dynamic? How do you know?

3. In Exercise 1.3, what is the effect of turning off Internet Explorer Enhanced Security Configuration?

LAB CHALLENGE: USING DISKPART.EXE

Completion time	15 minutes

Your supervisor wants to use the Windows Server 2008 Server Core option to deploy servers on the network. This means that most of the graphical system administration tools will not be available on these computers, so you have to brush up your command prompt skills. You must extend the spanned volume you created in Exercise 1.2 (Data2) to use all of the available disk space on Disk 1. However, you cannot use the Disk Management snap-in; you must use only the Diskpart.exe command-prompt utility.

To complete this challenge, write a procedure for completing your task, including all of the needed Diskpart commands. When you have successfully extended the spanned volume, open the Disk Management snap-in, and take a screen shot showing the volumes on the computer. Paste the image on the page provided in the lab01_worksheet file.

LAB 2
DEPLOYING A
FILE SERVER

This lab contains the following exercises and activities:

Exercise 2.1   Installing File Server Roles and Features

Exercise 2.2   Creating a Folder Share

Exercise 2.3   Testing Share Access

Exercise 2.4   Working with NTFS Permissions

Exercise 2.5   Using Share and Storage Management

Lab Review   Questions

Lab Challenge   Using Folder Redirection

BEFORE YOU BEGIN

The classroom network consists of Windows Server 2008 student servers and the ServerDC connected to a local area network. ServerDC, the domain controller for the contoso.com domain, is running Windows Server 2008. Throughout the labs in this manual, you will install, configure, maintain, and troubleshoot application roles, features, and services on the same student server.

To accommodate various types of classroom arrangements, each lab in this manual assumes that the student servers are in their baseline configuration, as described in Lab 1, "Preparing an Application Server." If you have not done so already, complete the initial configuration tasks in Exercise 1.1 of Lab 1 before beginning this lab.

Your instructor should have supplied the information needed to complete the following table.

Student computer name (Server##)	
Student account name (Student##)	

To complete the exercises in this lab, you must access a second student computer on the classroom network, referred to in the exercises as your *partner server*. Depending on the network configuration, use one of the following options as directed by your instructor:

- For a conventional classroom network with one operating system installed on each computer, your lab partner must perform the same exercises on his or her computer, known as your partner server.

- For a classroom in which each computer uses local virtualization software to install multiple operating systems, you must perform the exercises separately on two virtual machines representing your student server and your partner server.

- For a classroom using online virtualization, you must perform the exercises separately on two virtual student servers, representing your student server and your partner server, in your Web browser.

Working with Lab Worksheets

Each lab in this manual requires that you answer questions, save images of your screen, or perform other activities that you document in a worksheet named for the lab, such as *lab02_worksheet*. Your instructor placed the worksheet files in the Students\Worksheets share on ServerDC. As you perform the exercises in each lab, open the appropriate worksheet file using WordPad, fill in the required information, and save the file to your computer's Student##\Documents folder. This folder is automatically redirected to the ServerDC computer. Your instructor will examine these worksheet files to assess your performance.

The procedure for opening and saving a worksheet file is as follows:

1. Click Start, and then click Run. The Run dialog box appears.

2. In the Open text box, key **\\ServerDC\Students\Worksheets\lab##_worksheet** (where lab## contains the number of the lab you're completing), and click OK. The worksheet document opens in WordPad.

3. Complete all of the exercises in the worksheet.

4. In WordPad, choose Save As from the File menu. The Save As dialog box appears.

5. In the File Name text box, key **lab##_worksheet_*yourname*** (where lab## contains the number of the lab you're completing, and *yourname* is your last name), and click Save.

SCENARIO

You are a new administrator for Contoso, Ltd., working on a test deployment of the application server technologies included with Windows Server 2008. In this lab, you prepare a new computer for deployment as a file server.

After completing this lab, you will be able to:

■ Create a shared folder

■ Configure NTFS and share permissions

■ Use the Share and Storage Management snap-in

■ Map drives and redirect folders

Estimated lab time: 100 minutes

Exercise 2.1	Installing File Server Roles and Features
Overview	In this exercise, install the roles and features you will need to complete the exercises in this lab.
Completion time	10 minutes

1. Turn on your computer. When the logon screen appears, log on using your *Student##* account and the password *P@ssw0rd*. The Initial Configuration Tasks window appears.

2. Close the Initial Configuration Tasks window.

> **NOTE** *If your server already has the File Services role and the Group Policy Management and Active Directory Domain Services features installed from Lab 1, you can proceed immediately to Exercise 2.2.*

3. Open Server Manager, and install the File Services role, selecting the following role services:

   - File Server

   - Services for Network File System

4. When the role installation is complete, start the Add Features Wizard, and install the following features:

    • Group Policy Management

    • Remote Server Administration Tools > Role Administration Tools > Active Directory Domain Services Tools

> **NOTE**
>
> *To review the process of installing roles and features, see Exercises 1.3 and 1.4 in Lab 1, "Preparing an Application Server."*

5. Restart the computer when the feature installation is complete.

Exercise 2.2	Creating a Folder Share
Overview	Contoso, Ltd. documented a procedure for creating file server shares, which your supervisor insists that you follow. In this exercise, you create and share a folder in which Accounting department network users will store their spreadsheets using the company method.
Completion time	15 minutes

1. Log on to Windows Server 2008 using your *Student##* account and the password *P@ssw0rd*.

2. Click Start > All Programs > Accessories > Windows Explorer. The Windows Explorer window appears.

3. In Windows Explorer, expand the Computer container and, on the C: drive, create a new folder named **Accounting**.

4. Select the new Accounting folder. Right-click anywhere in the contents pane and, from the context menu, select New > Rich Text Document. Name the file **Budget**, and double-click it to open the file in WordPad.

5. Key text in the file. Save the file, and close the WordPad window.

6. Right-click the Accounting folder and, from the context menu, select Properties. The Accounting Properties sheet appears.

7. Click the Sharing tab, as shown in Figure 2-1.

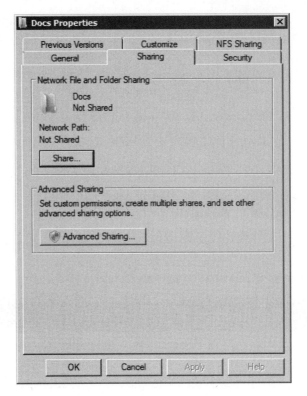

Figure 2-1
Sharing tab of a folder's Properties sheet

8. Click Advanced Sharing. In the User Account Control message box, click Continue to display the Advanced Sharing dialog box.

9. Select the Share This Folder checkbox.

10. In the Share Name text box, change the default value (Accounting) to **Spreadsheets**.

11. Click Permissions. The Permissions For Spreadsheets dialog box appears.

12. For the Everyone special identity, clear all checkboxes in the Allow column.

13. Click Add. The Select Users, Computers, Or Groups dialog box appears.

14. In the Enter The Object Names To Select box, key **Domain Admins**, and click OK. The Domain Admins group appears in the Group Or User Names list in the Permissions For Spreadsheets dialog box.

Question 1	What default share permissions does a group receive when it is added?

15. With the Domain Admins group highlighted, select the Full Control checkbox in the Allow column. This automatically selects the Change checkbox as well.

16. Using the same technique, add the Domain Users group to the Group Or User Names list, and assign only the Allow Read permission to it.

17. Press Ctrl+Prt Scr to take a screen shot of the Permissions For Spreadsheets dialog box. Press Ctrl+V to paste the image on the page provided in the lab02_worksheet file.

18. Click OK to close the Permissions For Spreadsheets dialog box.

19. Click OK to close the Advanced Sharing dialog box.

20. Click Close to close the Accounting Properties sheet.

21. Leave the computer logged on for the next exercise.

Exercise 2.3	Testing Share Access
Overview	To confirm that the folder share you created in Exercise 2.2 is operational, create a test user account, and connect to the share from another computer on the network.
Completion time	15 minutes

1. Click Start, and then click Administrative Tools > Active Directory Users And Computers. In the User Account Control message box, click Continue to display the Active Directory Users And Computers console.

2. Expand the contoso.com domain, and select the Users container, as shown in Figure 2-2.

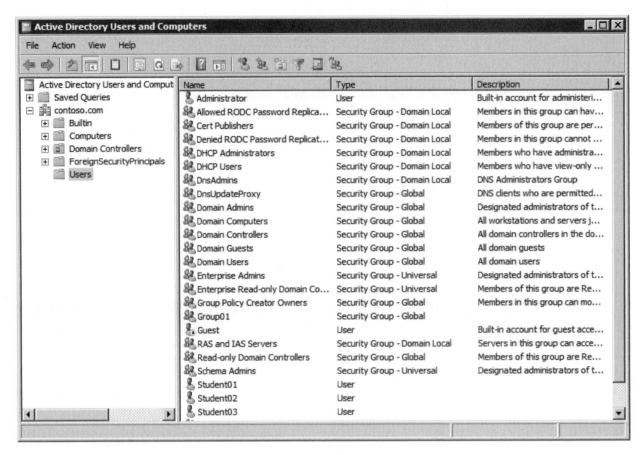

Figure 2-2
Active Directory Users And Computers console

3. Right-click the Users container and, on the context menu, click New > User. The New Object – User wizard appears.

4. In the First Name and User Logon Name text boxes, key **User##**, where ## is the number assigned to your computer.

5. Click Next. On the next page, key **P@ssw0rd** in the Password and Confirm Password text boxes.

6. Clear the User Must Change Password At Next Logon checkbox, and select the Password Never Expires checkbox. Click Next.

7. Click Finish to create the new user object.

8. Right-click the Users container and, on the context menu, click New > Group. The New Object – Group wizard appears.

9. In the Group Name text box, key **Group##**, where ## is the number assigned to your computer.

10. Click OK to create the new group object.

11. In the Users container, double-click the User## object you created. The User## Properties sheet appears.

12. Click the Member Of tab.

Question 2	*Identify the groups to which the User## object is assigned automatically.*

13. Click Add. The Select Groups dialog box appears.

14. In the Enter The Object Names To Select text box, key **Group##**. Click OK. Group## is added to the Member Of list.

15. Press Ctrl+Prt Scr to take a screen shot of the Member Of tab on the User## Properties sheet. Press Ctrl+V to paste the image on the page provided in the lab02_worksheet file.

16. Click OK to close the User## Properties sheet.

17. Move to your partner server on the classroom network, and log on to the domain with the *User##* account you created and the password *P@ssw0rd*.

NOTE	*In a conventional classroom environment, use another student's computer. In a virtual machine environment, use a different virtual machine on your computer.*

18. Open Windows Explorer, and browse to the Network container. A banner appears at the top of the window warning you that Network Discovery is turned off.

19. Click the banner and, from the context menu, select Turn On Network Discovery And File Sharing. The User Account Control message box is displayed.

20. In the User Name text box, key **contoso\administrator**. In the Password text box, key **P@ssw0rd**, and then click OK. The banner disappears, and the other network computers appear in the Network container.

> **NOTE**
>
> *In a conventional classroom environment, you might have to wait a few minutes until the other students complete this procedure before you see their computers on the network. In a virtual machine environment, you will not see your partner server on the network until you complete this procedure on the other virtual machine.*

21. Browse to the new Spreadsheets share on your own computer, and double-click the Budget file to open it.

22. Try to modify the text in the Budget file, and click File > Save.

Question 3	*What is the result?*

23. Close the Budget file without saving it. Select the Budget file if necessary, and press the Delete key.

Question 4	*What is the result?*
Question 5	*Why are you unable to modify or delete the Budget file?*

24. Log off of your partner server, and log on again, this time using your *Student##* account.

25. Try to open the Budget file again, modify the text, and save the file.

Question 6	*What is the result?*
Question 7	*Why are you able to modify the Budget file?*

26. Log off of your partner server.

27. Return to your server, and close the Active Directory Users And Computers console.

28. Leave the server logged on for the next exercise.

Exercise 2.4	Working with NTFS Permissions
Overview	After you create a share, the Contoso procedure requires you to protect the shared files using NTFS permissions. In this exercise, experiment with various combinations of permissions to control access to your shared files.
Completion time	15 minutes

1. Click Start > Accessories > Windows Explorer. The Windows Explorer window appears.

2. In Windows Explorer, expand the Computers container and the Local Disk (C:) drive.

3. Right-click the Accounting folder you created in Exercise 2.2 and, from the context menu, select Properties. The Accounting Properties sheet appears.

4. Click the Security tab, as shown in Figure 2-3.

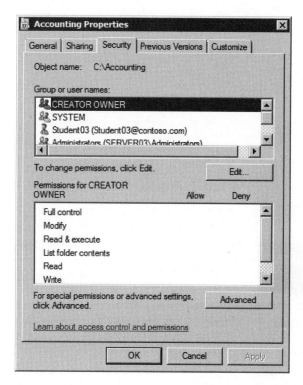

Figure 2-3
Security tab of the Accounting Properties sheet

Question 8	What NTFS permissions are explicitly assigned to the Student## user for the C:\Accounting folder?

5. Click Edit. The Permissions For Accounting dialog box appears.

6. Click Add. The Select Users, Computers, Or Groups dialog box appears.

7. In the Enter The Object Names To Select text box, key **Group##**, where ## is the number you used when creating the group object in Exercise 2.3, and click OK. Group## appears in the Group Or User Names list in the Permissions For Accounting dialog box.

8. Select Group## in the Group Or User Names list. In the Permissions For Group## box, select the Allow Full Control checkbox, and click OK.

9. Click OK again to close the Accounting Properties sheet.

10. Move to your partner server, and log on to the domain with the *User##* account you created in Exercise 2.3 and the password *P@ssw0rd*.

NOTE	*In a conventional classroom environment, use a different student's computer. In a virtual machine environment, use a different virtual machine on your computer.*

11. Open Windows Explorer, and browse to the Spreadsheets share you created on your computer in Exercise 2.3.

12. Open the Budget file, modify the text, and try to save your changes.

Question 9	*What is the result?*
Question 10	*Why are you unable to modify the Budget file when you have the Allow Full Control NTFS permission?*

13. Log off of your partner server.

14. Back on your own computer, log on to the domain as *User##*, open Windows Explorer, and try to modify the Budget file in the C:\Accounting folder.

Question 11	*What is the result?*
Question 12	*Why are you able to modify the Budget file on this computer when you were unable to modify it on the other computer?*

15. Log off of your computer, and log on again, this time using your *Student##* account and the password *P@ssw0rd*.

16. In Windows Explorer, open the Properties sheet for the Accounting folder and, on the Sharing tab, open the Advanced Sharing dialog box.

17. Click Permissions to open the Permissions For Spreadsheets dialog box.

18. Add the Group## group you created to the Group Or User Names list, and assign the Allow Change share permission to it.

19. Return to your partner server, log on to the domain as *User##*, and try again to modify the Budget file in the Spreadsheets share.

Question 13	*What is the result?*
Question 14	*Why did granting the Allow Change permission to Group## enable the User## account to read and modify the Budget file?*

20. Log off of your partner server.

21. Contoso's sharing guidelines call for all access control to be performed using NTFS permissions, not share permissions. On your computer, modify the permissions for the C:\Accounting folder you created to conform to the settings shown in Table 2-1.

Table 2-1
Permissions

Group	*Share Permissions*	*NTFS Permissions*
Group##	Allow Full Control	• Allow Modify • Allow Read & execute • Allow List folder contents • Allow Read • Allow Write
Domain Users	Allow Full Control	• Allow Read & execute • Allow List folder contents • Allow Read
Domain Admins	Allow Full Control	• Allow Full Control

22. Press Ctrl+Prt Scr to take a screen shot of the Security tab on the Accounting Properties sheet, showing the NTFS permissions assigned to the Group## group. Press Ctrl+V to paste the image on the page provided in the lab02_worksheet file.

23. Leave the server logged on for the next exercise.

Exercise 2.5	Using Share and Storage Management
Overview	While examining the new features in Windows Server 2008, you discover the Share And Storage Management console, which can streamline the process of creating and managing shares and their permissions. In this exercise, convince your supervisor that Contoso should revise its sharing procedure to use this new tool.
Completion time	15 minutes

1. Click Start > Administrative Tools > Share And Storage Management. In the User Account Control message box, click Continue to display the Share And Storage Management console shown in Figure 2-4.

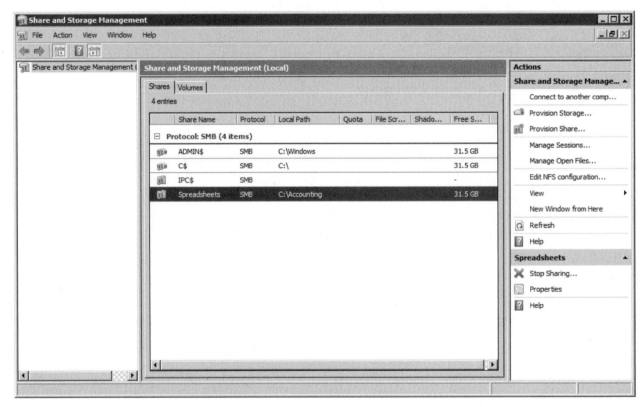

Figure 2-4
Share And Storage Management console

2. In the actions pane, click Provision Storage. The Provision Storage Wizard appears.

3. On the *Storage Source* page, click Next to accept the default One Or More Disks Available On This Server option. The *Disk Drive* page appears.

4. Select Disk 1, and click Next. The *Volume Size* page appears.

5. In the Specify A Size For The New Volume spin box, select a value that represents half the total size of Disk 1. Click Next. The *Volume Creation* page appears.

6. Leave the Assign Drive Letter To This Volume option selected and, from the drop-down list, select the drive letter X. Then click Next. The *Format* page appears.

7. In the Volume Label text box, key **Docs**. Leave the other default settings, and click Next. The *Review Settings And Create Storage* page appears.

8. Click Create. The wizard creates and formats the volume.

9. Click Close.

10. Press Ctrl+Prt Scr to take a screen shot of the Volumes tab in the Share And Storage Management console showing the volume you just created. Press Ctrl+V to paste the image on the page provided in the lab02_worksheet file.

11. Click Provision Share. The Provision A Shared Folder Wizard appears, displaying the *Shared Folder Location* page.

12. Click Browse. The Browse For Folder dialog box appears.

13. Select the x$ share, and click Make New Folder. Key **Docs**, and click OK. The x:\Docs path appears in the Location text box.

14. Click Next. The *NTFS Permissions* page appears.

15. Select the Yes, Change NTFS Permissions option, and click Edit Permissions. The Permissions For Docs dialog box appears.

16. Use Table 2-1 to assign the same NTFS permissions to the Docs folder that you assigned to the Accounting folder in Exercise 2.4. Then click OK.

17. Click Next. The *Share Protocols* page appears.

18. Select the SMB checkbox and, in the Share Name text box, key **Documents**.

19. Select the NFS checkbox and, in the Share Name text box, leave the default Docs value. Click Next. The *SMB Settings* page appears.

Question 15	*Why not use the same share name for the SMB and NFS protocols?*

20. Click Advanced. The Advanced dialog box appears.

21. Select the Enable Access-based Enumeration checkbox, and click OK.

22. Click Next. The *SMB Permissions* page appears.

23. Select the Users And Groups Have Custom Share Permissions option, and click Permissions. The Permissions For Documents dialog box appears.

24. Use Table 2-1 to assign the same share permissions to the Docs folder that you assigned to the Accounting folder in Exercise 2.4. Click OK.

25. Click Next. The *NFS Permissions* page appears.

26. In the Client Groups And Host Permissions box, select the ALL MACHINES entry, and click Edit. The Edit Client Group Or Host dialog box appears.

27. In the Permissions drop-down list, select Read-Write, and click OK.

28. Click Next. Then click Next again to bypass the *DFS Namespace Publishing* page. The *Review Settings And Create Share* page appears.

29. Click Create. The wizard creates the SMB and NFS shares.

30. Click Close.

31. Press Ctrl+Prt Scr to take a screen shot of the Shares tab of the Share And Storage Management console showing the two shares you just created. Press Ctrl+V to paste the image on the page provided in the lab02_worksheet file.

LAB REVIEW: QUESTIONS

Completion time   5 minutes

1. In Exercise 2.4, how could you tell which permissions were explicitly assigned to the Student## user for the C:\Accounting folder?

2. In Exercise 2.4, how did the Student## user obtain the NTFS permissions to the C:\Accounting folder that are explicitly assigned to it?

3. What command would you use in a logon script to map a user's Z: drive to the Documents share you created in Exercise 2.5?

LAB CHALLENGE: USING FOLDER REDIRECTION

Completion time   15 minutes

Your supervisor wants the Accounting users to store personal files on the server you just configured. To complete this challenge, create a new Group Policy Object (GPO), named after your Student## account and linked to the contoso.com domain, that redirects the Documents folder for all members of your Group## group to the Documents share you created in Exercise 2.5. Write the steps of your procedure in the space provided in the lab02_worksheet file.

LAB 3
USING THE FILE SERVICES ROLE

This lab contains the following exercises and activities:

Exercise 3.1   Creating a Standalone DFS Namespace

Exercise 3.2   Adding a Folder to a Namespace

Exercise 3.3   Testing Standalone Namespace Access

Exercise 3.4   Creating a Domain-based Namespace

Exercise 3.5   Adding a Namespace Server

Lab Review   Questions

Lab Challenge   Configuring DFS Replication

Workstation Reset   Return to Baseline

BEFORE YOU BEGIN

The classroom network consists of Windows Server 2008 student servers and the ServerDC connected to a local area network. ServerDC, the domain controller for the contoso.com domain, is running Windows Server 2008. Throughout the labs in this manual, you will install, configure, maintain, and troubleshoot application roles, features, and services on the same student server.

To accommodate various types of classroom arrangements, each lab in this manual assumes that the student servers are in their baseline configuration, as described in Lab 1, "Preparing an Application Server." If you have not done so already, complete the initial configuration tasks in Exercise 1.1 of Lab 1 before beginning this lab.

Your instructor should have supplied the information needed to complete the following table.

Student computer name (Server##)	
Student account name (Student##)	

To complete the exercises in this lab, you must access a second student computer on the classroom network, referred to in the exercises as your *partner server*. Depending on the network configuration, use one of the following options, as directed by your instructor:

- For a conventional classroom network with one operating system installed on each computer, your lab partner must perform the same exercises on his or her computer, known as your partner server.

- For a classroom in which each computer uses local virtualization software to install multiple operating systems, you must perform the exercises separately on two virtual machines representing your student server and your partner server.

- For a classroom using online virtualization, you must perform the exercises separately on two virtual student servers, representing your student server and your partner server, in your Web browser.

Working with Lab Worksheets

Each lab in this manual requires that you answer questions, save images of your screen, or perform other activities that you document in a worksheet named for the lab, such as *lab03_worksheet*. Your instructor placed the worksheet files in the Students\Worksheets share on ServerDC. As you perform the exercises in each lab, open the appropriate worksheet file using WordPad, fill in the required information, and save the file to your computer's Student##\Documents folder. This folder is automatically redirected to the ServerDC computer. Your instructor will examine these worksheet files to assess your performance.

The procedure for opening and saving a worksheet file is as follows:

1. Click Start, and then click Run. The Run dialog box appears.

2. In the Open text box, key **\\ServerDC\Students\Worksheets\lab##_worksheet** (where lab## contains the number of the lab you're completing), and click OK. The worksheet document opens in WordPad.

3. Complete all of the exercises in the worksheet.

4. In WordPad, choose Save As from the File menu. The Save As dialog box appears.

5. In the File Name text box, key **lab##_worksheet_*yourname*** (where lab## contains the number of the lab you're completing, and *yourname* is your last name), and click Save.

SCENARIO

You are a new administrator for Contoso, Ltd., working on a test deployment of the application server technologies included with Windows Server 2008. In this lab, you examine the capabilities of the Distributed File System.

After completing this lab, you will be able to:

- Create a standalone DFS namespace

- Add folders to a namespace

- Create a domain-based DFS namespace

- Create additional namespace servers

- Configure DFS replication

Estimated lab time: 100 minutes

Exercise 3.1	Creating a Standalone DFS Namespace
Overview	Contoso, Ltd. branch office users do not understand how networks and servers function. By creating a standalone DFS namespace on a server at each of these offices, you plan to consolidate the shares on multiple user workstations into a single entity accessible to the entire staff.
Completion time	15 minutes

1. Turn on your computer. When the logon screen appears, log on using your *Student##* account and the password *P@ssw0rd*.

2. Close the Initial Configuration Tasks window.

3. Open Server Manager, and start the Add Roles Wizard.

> **NOTE** *If your server already has the File Services role installed, start the Add Role Services Wizard instead, and add the DFS role services listed in the following steps.*

4. Click Next to bypass the *Before You Begin* page. The *Select Server Roles* page appears.

5. Select the File Services checkbox, and click Next.

6. Click Next again to bypass the File Services introductory page. The *Select Role Services* page appears.

7. Select the following role services, as shown in Figure 3-1, and click Next. The *Create A DFS Namespace* page appears.

    - File Server

    - Distributed File System > DFS Namespaces

    - Distributed File System > DFS Replication

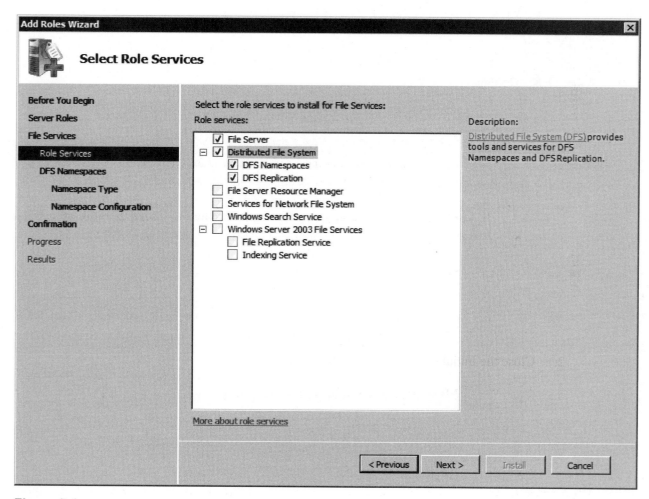

Figure 3-1
Select Role Services page in the Add Roles Wizard

8. Leave the Create A Namespace Now, Using This Wizard option selected and, in the Enter A Name For This Namespace text box, key **Data**. Then click Next. The *Select Namespace Type* page appears.

9. Select the Stand-alone Namespace option, and click Next. The *Configure Namespace* page appears.

Question 1	*What is the path to the DFS namespace you are creating, using the Universal Naming Convention (UNC) format?*

10. Click Add. The Add Folder To Namespace dialog box appears.

11. Click Browse. The Browse For Shared Folders dialog box appears.

12. Click Show Shared Folders. No shared folders appear in the Shared folders list.

NOTE	*If shared folders from a previous lesson appear, you can safely ignore them.*

13. Click New Shared Folder. The Create Share dialog box appears.

14. Click Browse. The Browse For Folder dialog box appears.

15. Select C$, and click Make New Folder. Key **Data##**, where ## is the number assigned to your computer, and click OK. The folder C:\Data## appears in the Local Path Of Shared Folder text box in the Create Share dialog box.

16. In the Share Name text box, key **Data##**.

17. Select the Administrators Have Full Access; Other Users Have Read And Write Permissions option, and click OK. The new shared folder appears in the Shared Folders box on the Browse For Shared Folders dialog box.

Question 2	*What share permissions does your Student## user have to the Data## share you just created?*
Question 3	*How did the Student## user receive those share permissions?*

18. Select the shared folder you created, and click OK. The share appears in the Add Folder To Namespace dialog box.

19. Leave the default Data## name in the Step 2 text box, and click OK. The Data## share appears in the Namespace box on the *Configure Namespace* page.

20. Press Ctrl+Prt Scr to take a screen shot of the *Configure Namespace* page showing your Data## share. Press Ctrl+V to paste the image on the page provided in the lab03_worksheet file.

21. Click Next. The *Confirm Installation Selections* page appears.

22. Click Install. When the File Services role is installed, click Close.

23. Close any open windows and leave the computer logged on for the next exercise.

Exercise 3.2	Adding a Folder to a Namespace
Overview	After you create a standalone DFS namespace, you can add shared folders from any computer on the network, making them accessible through the namespace.
Completion time	5 minutes

1. Click Start, and then click Administrative Tools > DFS Management. Click Continue in the User Account Control message box to display the DFS Management console. Select the Namespaces node as shown in Figure 3-2.

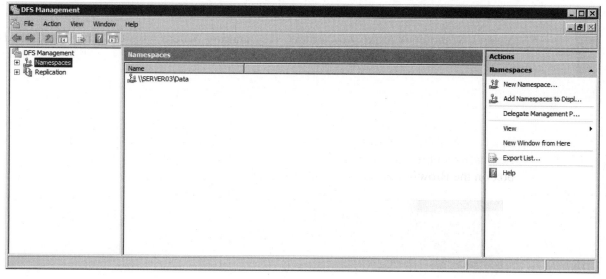

Figure 3-2
DFS Management console

2. Expand the Namespaces node, and select the Data namespace you created in Exercise 3.1.

<table>
<tr><td rowspan="1">NOTE</td><td>*Your server and your partner server must complete Exercise 3.1 before you continue with Exercise 3.2 so that each server has its own DFS namespace. At the end of Exercise 3.2, your server will have your partner server's share added to its namespace, and your partner server's namespace will have your share added to it.*</td></tr>
</table>

3. In the actions pane, select New Folder. The New Folder dialog box appears.

4. Click Add. The Add Folder target dialog box appears.

5. Click Browse. The Browse For Shared Folders dialog box appears.

6. In the Server text box, key the name of your partner server, and click Show Shared Folders.

<table>
<tr><td>Question 4</td><td>*How many shared folders appear in the Browse For Shared Folders dialog box for your partner server?*</td></tr>
<tr><td>Question 5</td><td>*How were the shares on your partner server created?*</td></tr>
</table>

7. Select the Data## share, and click OK. The path to the share appears in the Add Folder Target dialog box.

8. Click OK. The share appears in the New Folder dialog box.

9. In the Name text box, key **Data##**, where ## is the number assigned to your partner server. Then click OK. The new folder appears on the Namespace tab in the console.

10. Press Ctrl+Prt Scr to take a screen shot of the DFS Management console showing both of the shared folders in your namespace. Press Ctrl+V to paste the image on the page provided in the lab03_worksheet file.

11. Close the DFS Management console, and leave the computer logged on for the next exercise.

Exercise 3.3	Testing Standalone Namespace Access
Overview	To test a standalone namespace, access it by using the server name and the name you assigned to the namespace.
Completion time	10 minutes

1. Open Windows Explorer, and browse to the C:\Data## folder you created in Exercise 3.1.

2. Right-click in the detail (right) pane and, in the context menu, click New > Folder.

3. Key **Statistics##**, where ## is the number assigned to your computer, and press Enter to name the folder.

4. Select the folder you created, right-click in the detail pane and, in the context menu, click New > Rich Text Document.

5. Key **Budget##**, where ## is the number assigned to your computer, and press Enter to name the file.

6. Click Start, and then click Run. The Run dialog box appears.

7. In the Open text box, key **\\Server##\Data**, where ## is the number assigned to your partner server.

> **NOTE**
>
> *Before you continue with this exercise, verify that Exercise 3.2 has been completed on your partner server.*

8. Click OK. An Explorer window appears, displaying the Data namespace on your partner server.

> **Question 6**   *How many folders appear in the Data namespace?*

9. Press Ctrl+Prt Scr to take a screen shot of the Explorer window showing the Data namespace on your partner server and its folders. Press Ctrl+V to paste the image on the page provided in the lab03_worksheet file.

10. Open the Data## folder named for your server, expand the Statistics folder, and double-click the Budget file to open it in WordPad.

11.   Key text in the Budget file, and click File > Save.

Question 7	Which computer is hosting the DFS namespace you are accessing?
Question 8	On which computer are you saving the modified version of the Budget file?

12.   In Windows Explorer, open the C:\DfsRoots\Data folder.

13.   Double-click the Data## folder named for your partner server.

Question 9	What happens?

14.   Double-click the Data## folder named for your own server.

Question 10	What happens this time?
Question 11	How can you explain these results?

15.   Close the two Explorer windows, and leave the server logged on for the next exercise.

Exercise 3.4 Creating a Domain-based Namespace

Overview	In the Contoso, Ltd. headquarters, you will create a larger DFS installation that takes advantage of Active Directory Domain Services.
Completion time	10 minutes

1. Open the DFS Management console.

2. Select the Namespace node and, in the actions pane, click New Namespace. The New Namespace Wizard appears, displaying the *Namespace Server* page shown in Figure 3-3.

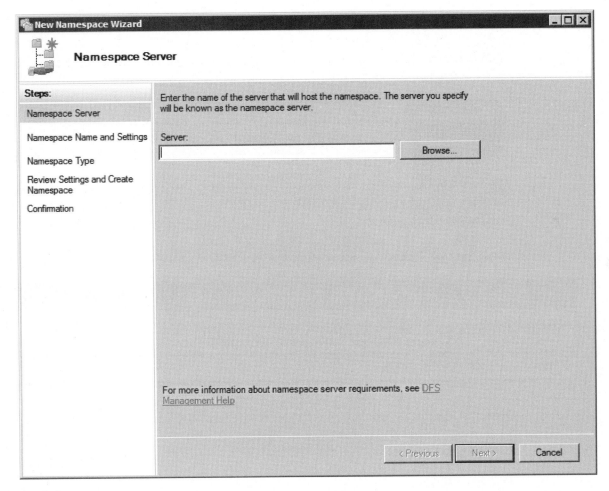

Figure 3-3
New Namespace Wizard in the DFS Management console

3. In the Server text box, key **Server##**, where ## is the number assigned to your server, and click Next. The *Namespace Name And Settings* page appears.

4. In the Name text box, key **Docs##**, where ## is the number assigned to your server.

5. Click Edit Settings. The Edit Settings dialog box appears.

6. Select the Administrators Have Full Access; Other Users Have Read And Write Permissions option, and click OK. Then click Next. The *Namespace Type* page appears.

7. Leave the Domain-based Namespace option selected, and click Next. The *Review Settings And Create Namespace* page appears.

8. Click Create. The wizard creates the namespace.

9. Click Close. The Docs## namespace appears in the DFS Management console.

10. Select the Docs## namespace and, in the actions pane, click New Folder.

11. Add the Data## shared folders on your server and your partner server, which you created earlier in this lab, to the Docs## namespace.

Question 12	On this domain-based namespace, where are the files appearing in the two Data## shares stored?

12. Press Ctrl+Prt Scr to take a screen shot of the DFS Management console showing the Docs## namespace and its folders. Press Ctrl+V to paste the image on the page provided in the lab03_worksheet file.

13. Leave the DFS Management console open for the next exercise.

Exercise 3.5	Adding a Namespace Server
Overview	Designate multiple namespace servers for fault tolerance, an advantage of using a domain-based DFS namespace.
Completion time	15 minutes

1. Open the Run dialog box and, in the Open text box, key **\\contoso\Docs##**, where ## is the number assigned to your server. Then click OK. An Explorer window appears, displaying the Docs## namespace you created.

Question 13	Where are the target folders for the namespace displayed in the Explorer window stored?

> **NOTE**
> *If you are working with a lab partner for steps 2–7 in this exercise, you will take turns shutting down your servers momentarily and using each others' servers to access your namespaces.*

2. Shut down your partner server for a few minutes.

3. On your computer, try to open the two Data## folders on your Docs## namespace.

    > **Question 14**
    > *How is access to your Docs## namespace impaired while your partner server is shut down?*

4. Restart your partner server, and shut down your own server.

5. At your partner server, log on using your *Student##* account and the password *P@ssw0rd*.

6. Try to access your Docs## namespace by opening the \\contoso\Docs## path from the Run dialog box.

    > **Question 15**
    > *How is access to your Docs## namespace affected while your server is shut down?*

7. Log off of your partner server, and restart your own server.

8. Log on to your server using your *Student##* account and the password *P@ssw0rd*.

9. Open the DFS Management console, and expand the Namespaces node.

10. Select the Data namespace you created in Exercise 3.1.

    > **Question 16**
    > *Explain why the Add Namespace Server command does not appear in the actions pane.*

11. Select the Docs## namespace you created in Exercise 3.4 and, in the actions pane, click Add Namespace Server. The Add Namespace Server dialog box appears, as shown in Figure 3-4.

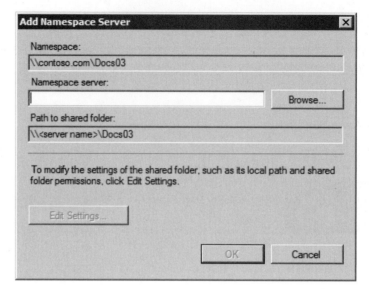

Figure 3-4
Add Namespace Server dialog box

12. In the Namespace Server text box, key **Server##**, where ## identifies your partner server.

13. Click Edit Settings. The Edit Settings dialog box appears.

14. Select the Administrators Have Full Access; Other Users Have Read And Write Permissions option, and click OK. Then, in the Add Namespace Server dialog box, click OK again.

15. In the DFS Management console, select the Namespace Servers tab.

16. Press Ctrl+Prt to take a screen shot of the DFS Management console showing the two namespace servers in your Docs## namespace. Press Ctrl+V to paste the image on the page provided in the lab03_worksheet file.

17. Shut down your server, and try again to access the two folders in your Docs## namespace from your partner server.

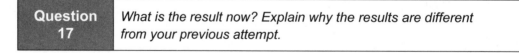

Question 17	What is the result now? Explain why the results are different from your previous attempt.

18. Restart your server.

LAB REVIEW: QUESTIONS

Completion time	5 minutes

1. You can create a domain-based namespace instead of a standalone namespace to suppress the server name in the namespace path. Why is suppressing the server name an advantage?

2. In Exercise 3.1, explain why it is not a problem for your server and your partner server to have DFS namespaces with the same name (Data).

3. In Exercise 3.3, you accessed the DFS namespace on your partner server and modified a file called Budget. Explain why the file you modified was actually stored on your own server rather than the partner server.

4. In Exercise 3.4, when you are creating the domain-based namespace, why is the Enable Windows Server 2008 Mode checkbox grayed out?

LAB CHALLENGE: CONFIGURING DFS REPLICATION

Completion time	15 minutes

In Exercise 3.5, you added a second namespace server to your domain-based namespace so the namespace remains available if one server fails. However, even though the namespace would remain available in the event of a server failure, one of the shared folders in the namespace would not be available. To make the data folders in the namespace fault tolerant as well, you can use DFS Replication to duplicate each folder on the other server.

To complete this challenge, use the DFS Management console to configure your Docs## namespace to be fully fault tolerant, using DFS Replication so that all resources remain available when one server fails. List the steps for the procedure to configure the namespace, and take a screen shot of the DFS Management console demonstrating that the Docs## namespace is using DFS Replication. Paste the image on the page provided in the lab03_worksheet file.

> **NOTE**
> *To avoid conflicts with your partner server, do not use the same folder name when replicating your folders to the other server. For example, when replicating Data01 to your partner server, call the folder Data01a.*

WORKSTATION RESET: RETURN TO BASELINE

Completion time	10 minutes

After this lab, you will no longer need the File Services role installed in your server. To return the computer to its baseline state, complete the following procedures.

1. Open the DFS Management console, and delete the namespaces you created during this lab.

2. Open the Share And Storage Management console, and delete all of the shares you created during Labs 1 to 3.

3. Open Windows Explorer, and delete all of the folders you created during Labs 1 to 3.

4. Open the Server Manager console, and remove the File Services role.

LAB 4
USING THE PRINT SERVICES ROLE

This lab contains the following exercises and activities:

Exercise 4.1	Installing a Printer
Exercise 4.2	Deploying Printers Using Active Directory
Exercise 4.3	Scheduling Printer Access
Exercise 4.4	Managing Queued Print Jobs
Lab Review	Questions
Lab Challenge	Creating a Printer Pool
Workstation Reset	Return to Baseline

BEFORE YOU BEGIN

The classroom network consists of Windows Server 2008 student servers and the ServerDC connected to a local area network. ServerDC, the domain controller for the contoso.com domain, is running Windows Server 2008. Throughout the labs in this manual, you will install, configure, maintain, and troubleshoot application roles, features, and services on the same student server.

To accommodate various types of classroom arrangements, each lab in this manual assumes that the student servers are in their baseline configuration, as described in Lab 1, "Preparing an Application Server." If you have not done so already, complete the initial configuration tasks in Exercise 1.1 of Lab 1 before beginning this lab.

Your instructor should have supplied the information needed to complete the following table:

Student computer name (Server##)	
Student account name (Student##)	

To complete the exercises in this lab, you must access a second student computer on the classroom network, referred to in the exercises as your *partner server*. Depending on the network configuration, use one of the following options, as directed by your instructor:

- For a conventional classroom network with one operating system installed on each computer, your lab partner must perform the same exercises on his or her computer, known as your partner server.

- For a classroom in which each computer uses local virtualization software to install multiple operating systems, you must perform the exercises separately on two virtual machines representing your student server and your partner server.

- For a classroom using online virtualization, you must perform the exercises separately on two virtual student servers, representing your student server and your partner server, in your Web browser.

Working with Lab Worksheets

Each lab in this manual requires that you answer questions, save images of your screen, or perform other activities that you document in a worksheet named for the lab, such as *lab04_worksheet*. Your instructor placed the worksheet files in the Students\Worksheets share on ServerDC. As you perform the exercises in each lab, open the appropriate worksheet file using WordPad, fill in the required information, and save the file to your computer's Student##\Documents folder. This folder is automatically redirected to the ServerDC computer. Your instructor will examine these worksheet files to assess your performance.

The procedure for opening and saving a worksheet file is as follows:

1. Click Start, and then click Run. The Run dialog box appears.

2. In the Open text box, key **\\ServerDC\Students\Worksheets\lab##_worksheet** (where lab## contains the number of the lab you're completing), and click OK. The worksheet document opens in WordPad.

3. Complete all of the exercises in the worksheet.

4. In WordPad, choose Save As from the File menu. The Save As dialog box appears.

5. In the File Name text box, key **lab##_worksheet_*yourname*** (where lab## contains the number of the lab you're completing and *yourname* is your last name), and click Save.

SCENARIO

You are a new administrator for Contoso, Ltd., working on a test deployment of the application server technologies included with Windows Server 2008. In this lab, you examine the capabilities of the Print Services role.

After completing this lab, you will be able to:

- Use the Print Management console

- Install a printer

- Deploy printers to workstations

- Control access to printers

- Manage queued print jobs

Estimated lab time: 75 minutes

Exercise 4.1	Installing a Printer
Overview	On your test network, you are examining the capabilities of the Print Management console included in Windows Server 2008. In this exercise, install the Print Services role, and use the Print Management console to install test printers.
Completion time	15 minutes

1. Turn on your computer. When the logon screen appears, log on using your *Student##* account and the password *P@ssw0rd*.

2. Close the Initial Configuration Tasks window.

3. Open Server Manager, and start the Add Roles Wizard.

4. Click Next to bypass the *Before You Begin* page. The *Select Server Roles* page appears.

5. Select the Print Services checkbox, and click Next.

6. Click Next again to bypass the Print Services introductory page. The *Select Role Services* page appears.

7. Select the Print Server role service, and click Next. The *Confirm Installation Selections* page appears.

8. Click Install. When the Print Services role is installed, click Close.

9. Click Start, and then click Administrative Tools > Print Management. Click Continue in the User Account Control message box to display the Print Management console, shown in Figure 4-1.

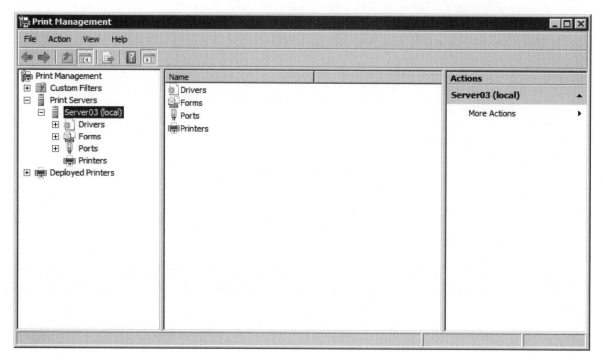

Figure 4-1
Print Management console

10. Expand the Print Servers node, and then right-click the Server## (local) node representing your computer. From the context menu, select Add Printer. The Network Printer Installation Wizard appears.

11. Select the Add A New Printer Using An Existing Port option, and leave the LPT1: (Printer Port) value selected. Then click Next. The *Printer Driver* page appears.

12. Leave the Install A New Driver option selected, and click Next. The *Printer Installation* page appears.

13. In the Manufacturer list, select Generic.

14. In the Printers list, select MS Publisher Color Printer, and click Next. The *Printer Name And Sharing Settings* page appears.

15. In the Printer Name text box, key **MSColor##**, where ## is the number assigned to your computer.

16. Leave the Share This Printer checkbox selected and, in the Share Name text box, key **MSColor##**. Then click Next. The *Printer Found* page appears.

Question 1	Why is the wizard able to install the printer when an actual print device is not connected to the computer?

17. Click Next. The *Completing The Network Printer Installation Wizard* page appears.

18. After the printer is installed, click Finish.

19. Repeat the process to install a second printer, using the following settings:

    - File Server

    - Port: LPT2

    - Manufacturer: Generic

    - Printer: MS Publisher Imagesetter

    - Printer Name: MSMono##, where ## is the number assigned to your computer

    - Share Name: MSMono##, where ## is the number assigned to your computer

20. Select the Printers node, under your print server, in the Print Management console.

21. Press Ctrl+Prt Scr to take a screen shot of the Print Management console showing the contents of the Printers node. Press Ctrl+V to paste the image on the page provided in the lab04_worksheet file.

22. Leave the computer logged on for the next exercise.

Exercise 4.2	Deploying Printers Using Active Directory
Overview	To simplify future network printer deployments, Contoso plans to publish printer connections using Active Directory and Group Policy. In this exercise, you use two methods to deploy the printers you created.
Completion time	15 minutes

1. In the Print Management console, expand the node representing your server, and select the Printers node beneath it.

2. Right-click the MSColor## printer and, from the context menu, select List In Directory.

3. Right-click the MSMono## printer and, from the context menu, select Deploy With Group Policy. The Deploy With Group Policy dialog box appears, as shown in Figure 4-2.

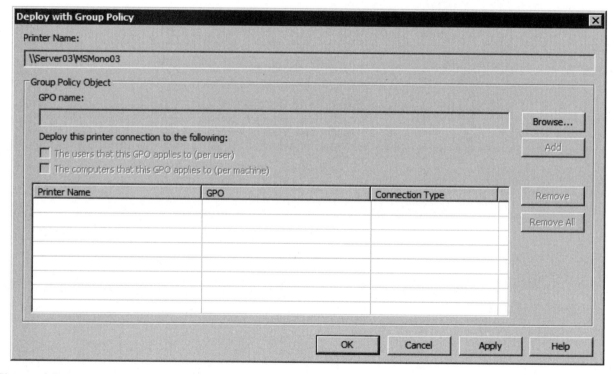

Figure 4-2
Deploy With Group Policy dialog box

4. Click Browse. The Browse For A Group Policy Object dialog box appears.

5. Select Default Domain Policy, and click OK. Default Domain Policy appears in the GPO Name field.

6. Select the checkbox for The Computers That This GPO Applies To (Per Machine), and click Add.

7. Click OK. A Print Management message box appears, indicating that the printer deployment has succeeded.

8. Click OK twice to close the Deploy With Group Policy dialog box.

9. When this exercise is complete to this point on both your server and your partner server, restart your computer.

10. Log on to your computer using your *Student##* account and the password *P@ssw0rd*.

11. Click Start, and then click Control Panel.

12. Double-click the Printers icon. The Printers window appears.

Question 2	Apart from Microsoft XPS Document Writer, which appears by default, which of your partner server's printers appear in the window?
Question 3	Explain why your partner server's MSColor## printer does not appear in the Printers window.

13. Press Ctrl+Prt Scr to take a screen shot of the Printers window. Press Ctrl+V to paste the image on the page provided in the lab04_worksheet file.

14. Click Start, and then click Network. The Network window appears.

15. Click Search Active Directory. The Find Users, Contacts, And Groups dialog box appears.

16. In the Find drop-down list, select Printers. The title of the dialog box changes to Find Printers.

17. Click Find Now.

Question 4	What printers appear in the Search Results box?

18. Right-click your partner server's MSColor## printer and, from the context menu, select Connect.

19. Switch to the Printers window.

Question 5	*What changed in the Printers window?*

20. Close the Printers window and the Network window. Leave the computer logged on for the next exercise.

Exercise 4.3   Scheduling Printer Access

Overview	Consumables for the color printer you installed in Exercise 4.1 are expensive, so you want to prevent users from running personal jobs or printing after hours. However, you want selected users to be able to access the printer at all times. You also want to prioritize those users' print jobs, printing them before other users' jobs.
	In this exercise, you create a second printer for the same print device and use it to provide priority access for a group of selected users.
Completion time	10 minutes

---

1. Open the Print Management console, and create a second printer for the MS Publisher Color Printer you installed in Exercise 4.1. Use the following settings:

   - Port: LPT1

   - Printer Driver: MS Publisher Color Printer

   - Manufacturer: Generic

   - Printer: MS Publisher Color Printer

   - Printer Name: MSColor##-PM, where ## is the number assigned to your computer

   - Share Name: MSColor##-PM, where ## is the number assigned to your computer

2. Select the Printers node in the console, right-click the MSColor## printer you created earlier and, in the context menu, select Properties. The MSColor## Properties sheet appears.

3. Click the Advanced tab, as shown in Figure 4-3.

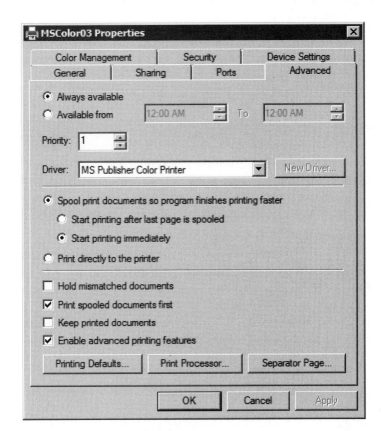

Figure 4-3
Advanced tab of a printer's Properties sheet

4. Select the Available From option and, in the two spin boxes, select the hours 9:00 AM and 5:00 PM.

Question 6	Which of the problems described in the Exercise 4.3 overview will this setting prevent? How is it prevented?

5. Click Apply, and then click the Security tab.

6. Add the Domain Users group to the Group Or User Names list, and grant the Allow Print permission to the group.

7. Remove the Everyone special identity from the Group Or User Names list.

8. Click OK to close the MSColor## Properties sheet.

9. Open the MSColor##-PM Properties sheet, and click the Advanced tab.

10. Leave the Always Available option selected, and change the value in the Priority spin box to 99.

Question 7	Which of the problems described in the Exercise 4.3 overview will be prevented by modifying the Priority value? How is it prevented?

11. Click Apply, and then click the Security tab.

12. Add the Domain Admins group to the Group Or User Names list, and grant the Allow Print permission to it.

13. Remove the Everyone special identity from the Group Or User Names list.

Question 8	How do these permission modifications achieve the goals stated in the exercise overview?

14. Press Ctrl+Prt Scr to take a screen shot of the Security tab in the MSColor##-PM Properties sheet. Press Ctrl+V to paste the image on the page provided in the lab04_worksheet file.

15. Leave the Print Management console open for the next exercise.

Exercise 4.4	Managing Queued Print Jobs
Overview	To test your network's printing capabilities, a group of users generate various types of print jobs. The users encountered several problems.
	When users send print jobs requiring a paper size that is not available, the entire print queue halts until someone inserts the correct paper for that job. In several instances, a user deliberately or accidently interrupted a print job, stalling the queue until the partial job was removed.
	In this exercise, modify a printer's settings to create a secure printing environment that prevents such print queue errors.
Completion time	10 minutes

1. In the Print Management console, open the Properties sheet for the MSMono## printer on your server, and click the Sharing tab.

2. Clear the Render Print Jobs On Client Computers checkbox, and click Apply.

3. Click the Advanced tab.

4.   Select the Start Printing After Last Page Is Spooled option.

Question 9	*Which of the problems described in the Exercise 4.4 overview will be prevented by selecting the Start Printing After Last Page Is Spooled option?*

5.   Select the Hold Mismatched Documents checkbox.

Question 10	*Which of the problems described in the Exercise 4.4 overview will be prevented by selecting the Hold Mismatched Documents option?*

6.   Click OK to close the MSMono## Properties sheet.

7.   Click Start, and then click Internet Explorer. An Internet Explorer window appears.

8.   Click the down arrow next to the Print button and, from the context menu, select Print. The Print dialog box appears.

9.   Select the MSMono## printer on your server, as shown in Figure 4-4, and click Print.

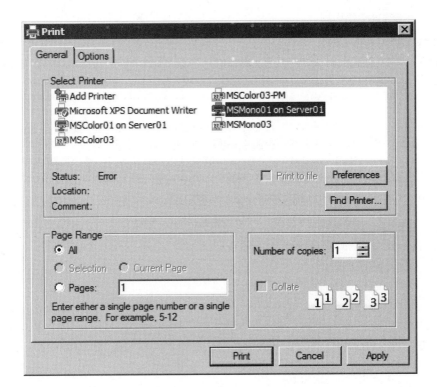

Figure 4-4
Print dialog box

10. Repeat steps 8 to 9 twice to print a total of three copies of the default Internet Explorer page on your MSMono## printer.

11. Print three more copies of the default Internet Explorer page on the MSMono## printer on your partner server.

Question 11	Why do error messages appear when you attempt to send print jobs to the MSMono## printer on your partner server?

12. In the Print Management console, expand the node representing your server, and select the MSMono## printer.

Question 12	What does the console tell you about the printer's current state?

13. Right-click the Printers node and, from the context menu, select Show Extended View.

Question 13	What happens?
Question 14	Explain why the three jobs you submitted to the printer on your partner server are not displayed.

14. Right-click the Print Servers node in the console and, from the context menu, select Add/Remove Servers. The Add/Remove Servers dialog box appears.

15. In the Add Server text box, key the name of your partner server, and click Add To List. Click OK. Your partner server appears in the console.

16. Expand the node representing your partner server. Then, select the Printers node beneath the server, and select the MSMono## printer.

Question 15	What do you see?

17. Press Ctrl+Prt Scr to take a screen shot of the Print Management console showing the jobs in your partner server's MSMono## print queue. Press Ctrl+V to paste the image on the page provided in the lab04_worksheet file.

LAB REVIEW QUESTIONS

Completion time	5 minutes

1. After you deployed the MSMono## printer using Group Policy, you noticed that the printer appears correctly on your network's Windows Vista computers but not on the Windows XP computers. Why is this the case, and how can you resolve the problem?

2. In Exercise 4.3, you removed the Everyone special identity and granted the Print permission to the Domain Users group. How do these changes enhance the printer's security?

3. In Exercise 4.4, does clearing the Print Jobs On Client Computers checkbox increase or decrease the processor burden on the server hosting the printer?

LAB CHALLENGE: CREATING A PRINTER POOL

Completion time	20 minutes

To support the Legal department at Contoso, Ltd., your supervisor purchased five identical HP LaserJet 4250 printers to be used as a printer pool. Unlike the printers you installed earlier in this lab, which connected to the server using LPT ports, these five printers have Hewlett Packard JetDirect network interface adapters that have already been assigned the following IP addresses:

- 10.1.1.220
- 10.1.1.221
- 10.1.1.222
- 10.1.1.223
- 10.1.1.224

To complete this challenge, create a printer on your server, and share it using the name HPLJ4250 Pool. Then, configure the printer to function as a printer pool using the IP addresses cited earlier. Write the procedure you use to create and configure the printer pool, and then take a screen shot of the Ports tab in the HPLJ4250 Pool Properties sheet. Paste the image in the lab04_worksheet file.

WORKSTATION RESET: RETURN TO BASELINE

Completion time	10 minutes

After this lab, you will no longer need the Print Services role installed in your server. To return the computer to its baseline state, complete the following procedures.

1. Open the Print Management console, and delete the printers you created during the lab.

2. Open the Server Manager console, and remove the Print Services role.

LAB 5
DEPLOYING A WEB SERVER

This lab contains the following exercises and activities:

BEFORE YOU BEGIN

The classroom network consists of Windows Server 2008 student servers and the ServerDC connected to a local area network. ServerDC, the domain controller for the contoso.com domain, is running Windows Server 2008. Throughout the labs in this manual, you will install, configure, maintain, and troubleshoot application roles, features, and services on the same student server.

To accommodate various types of classroom arrangements, each lab in this manual assumes that the student servers are in their baseline configuration, as described in Lab 1, "Preparing an Application Server." If you have not done so already, complete the initial configuration tasks in Exercise 1.1 of Lab 1 before beginning this lab.

Your instructor should have supplied the information needed to complete the following table:

Student computer name (Server##)	
Student account name (Student##)	

To complete the exercises in this lab, you must access a second student computer on the classroom network, referred to in the exercises as your *partner server*. Depending on the network configuration, use one of the following options, as directed by your instructor:

- For a conventional classroom network with one operating system installed on each computer, your lab partner must perform the same exercises on his or her computer, known as your partner server.

- For a classroom in which each computer uses local virtualization software to install multiple operating systems, you must perform the exercises separately on two virtual machines representing your student server and your partner server.

- For a classroom using online virtualization, you must perform the exercises separately on two virtual student servers, representing your student server and your partner server, in your Web browser.

Working with Lab Worksheets

Each lab in this manual requires that you answer questions, save images of your screen, or perform other activities that you document in a worksheet named for the lab, such as *lab05_worksheet*. Your instructor placed the worksheet files in the Students\Worksheets share on ServerDC. As you perform the exercises in each lab, open the appropriate worksheet file using WordPad, fill in the required information, and save the file to your computer's Student##\Documents folder. This folder is automatically redirected to the ServerDC computer. Your instructor will examine these worksheet files to assess your performance.

The procedure for opening and saving a worksheet file is as follows:

1. Click Start, and then click Run. The Run dialog box appears.

2. In the Open text box, key **\\ServerDC\Students\Worksheets\lab##_worksheet** (where lab## contains the number of the lab you're completing), and click OK. The worksheet document opens in WordPad.

3. Complete all of the exercises in the worksheet.

4. In WordPad, choose Save As from the File menu. The Save As dialog box appears.

5. In the File Name text box, key **lab##_worksheet_*yourname*** (where lab## contains the number of the lab you're completing and *yourname* is your last name), and click Save.

SCENARIO

You are a new administrator for Contoso, Ltd., working on a test deployment of the application server technologies included with Windows Server 2008. In this lab, you test the capabilities of the Web Server (IIS) role.

After completing this lab, you will be able to:

- Configure IIS7 properties at the server and site level

- Create Web sites

- Create virtual directories

- Configure site bindings

Estimated lab time: 85 minutes

Exercise 5.1	Installing the Web Server (IIS) Role
Overview	In this exercise, you install IIS7 by adding the Web Server (IIS) role to the computer.
Completion time	5 minutes

1. Turn on your computer. When the logon screen appears, log on using your *Student##* account and the password *P@ssw0rd*.

2. Close the Initial Configuration Tasks window.

3. Open Server Manager, and start the Add Roles Wizard.

4. Click Next to bypass the *Before You Begin* page. The *Select Server Roles* page appears.

5. Select the Web Server (IIS) checkbox. An Add Roles Wizard message box appears, listing the features required to add the Web Server (IIS) role.

Question 1	*Why is the Windows Process Activation Services needed to run the Web Server (IIS) role?*

6. Click Add Required Features, and then click Next. The *Introduction To Web Server (IIS)* page appears.

7. Click Next to bypass the introductory page. The *Select Role Services* page appears.

8. Click Next to accept the default role service selections. The *Confirm Installation Selections* page appears.

9. Click Install. The wizard installs the role.

10. Click Close.

11. Close Server Manager, and leave the computer logged on for the next exercise.

Exercise 5.2	Configuring Web Server Properties
Overview	Using the default Web site that Windows Server 2008 creates during the role installation, experiment with the various IIS7 site display options.
Completion time	15 minutes

1. Click Start, and then click Internet Explorer. An Internet Explorer window appears.

> **NOTE**
> *If the default Internet Explorer page states that Internet Explorer Enhanced Security Configuration is enabled, open Server Manager. In the Server Summary box under Security Information, click Configure IE ESC, and turn ESC off for Administrators.*

2. In the Address box, key **http://127.0.0.1**, and press Enter. An IIS7 splash page appears.

3. Click Start. Then click Administrative Tools > Internet Information Services (IIS) Manager. Click Continue in the User Account Control message box to display the Internet Information Services (IIS) Manager window, shown in Figure 5-1.

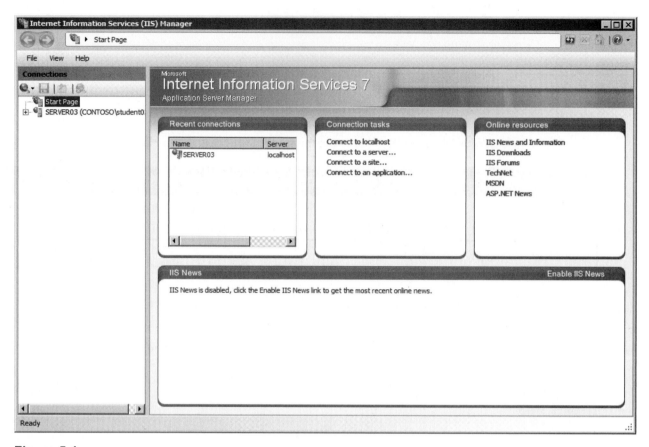

Figure 5-1
Internet Information Services (IIS) Manager window

4. Expand the Server## node representing your server. The *Server## Home* page appears in the middle pane.

5. Double-click the Default Document icon. The *Default Document* page appears in the middle pane.

6. Select the iisstart.htm file and, in the actions pane, click Remove. Then, click Yes to confirm the removal.

> **NOTE**
>
> *Removing a file from the Default Document page does not delete the file itself; it merely removes the file reference from the IIS7 configuration.*

7. Switch back to the Internet Explorer window, and click the Refresh button. An error message page appears, citing an HTTP Error 403.14.

<table>
<tr><td>**Question 2**</td><td>*What conclusion can you draw from this result?*</td></tr>
</table>

8. Press Ctrl+Prt Scr to take a screen shot of the Internet Explorer window showing the result of your page refresh. Press Ctrl+V to paste the image on the page provided in the lab05_worksheet file.

9. Open Windows Explorer, and browse to the C:\Inetpub\wwwroot folder.

10. Locate the iisstart file, and rename it **Default**. Click Continue when the User Account Control message box appears.

<table>
<tr><td>**Question 3**</td><td>*What do you predict will happen when you refresh the Internet Explorer page again? Why?*</td></tr>
</table>

11. Return to the Internet Information Services (IIS) Manager window. Click the back arrow to return to the *Server## Home* page.

12. Double-click the Directory Browsing icon. The *Directory Browsing* page appears.

13. In the actions pane, click Enable.

14. Return to the Windows Explorer window, and rename the Default file **iisstart**, the file's original name.

15. Refresh the Internet Explorer window.

<table>
<tr><td>**Question 4**</td><td>*What is the result this time? Why is the result different?*</td></tr>
</table>

16. Press Ctrl+Prt Scr to take a screen shot of the Internet Explorer window showing the result of your page refresh. Press Ctrl+V to paste the image on the page provided in the lab05_worksheet file.

17. In the Internet Information Services (IIS) Manager window, disable the Directory Browsing option, and click the back arrow to return to the *Server## Home* page.

18. Double-click the Error Pages icon. The *Error Pages* page appears.

19. In the actions pane, click Edit Feature Settings. The Edit Error Pages Settings dialog box appears.

20. Select the Custom Error Pages option, and click OK.

21. Refresh the Internet Explorer window.

Question 5	*How is this error message page different from the previous one?*

22. Press Ctrl+Prt Scr to take a screen shot of the Internet Explorer window showing the result of your page refresh. Press Ctrl+V to paste the image on the page provided in the lab05_worksheet file.

23. Open the Edit Error Pages Settings dialog box again, and select the Detailed Errors For Local Requests And Custom Error Pages For Remote Requests option. Then click OK.

24. Click the back arrow to return to the *Server## Home* page.

25. Open the *Default Document* page again and, in the actions pane, click Add. The Add Default Document dialog box appears.

26. In the Name text box, key **iisstart.htm**, and click OK.

27. Click the back arrow to return to the *Server## Home* page.

28. Refresh the Internet Explorer window one last time. The IIS7 splash page appears again.

29. Leave the computer logged on for the next exercise.

Exercise 5.3   Preparing Web Site Content

Overview	Before you can create new Web sites on your IIS7 server, you must have content to publish on them.
Completion time	15 minutes

1. Click Start. Then click All Programs > Accessories > Notepad. A Notepad window appears.

2. In the Notepad window, key the following text, replacing the ## with the number assigned to your server.

    ```
    <html><body>

    <h1><center>Contoso, Ltd.</center></h1>

    <h2><center>www##.contoso.com</center></h2>

    </html></body>
    ```

3. Click File > Save As. The Save As dialog box appears.

4. Click Browse Folders. The dialog box expands to display the contents of your Documents folder.

5. Click New Folder. Then, key **www##**, where ## is the number assigned to your server, and press Enter.

6. In the Save As Type drop-down list, select All Files.

7. In the File Name text box, key **Default.htm**, and click Save.

Question 6	*Why is it necessary to change the Save As Type value to All Files?*

8. Create another subfolder in your Documents folder called **Sales##**. Create a file inside it called **Default.htm**, containing the following text:

    ```
    <html><body>

    <h1><center>Contoso, Ltd. Sales</center></h1>

    <h2><center>sales##.contoso.com</center></h2>

    </html></body>
    ```

9. Close the Notepad window.

10. Open Server Manager, and select the Features node.

11. Click Add Features. The Add Features Wizard appears, displaying the *Select Features* page.

12. Browse to the Remote Server Administration Tools > Role Administration Tools node, and select the DNS Server Tools checkbox. Then, click Next. The *Confirm Installation Selections* page appears.

13. Click Install. The wizard installs the DNS Manager console.

14. Click Close, and then close the Server Manager console.

15. Click Start. Then, click Administrative Tools > DNS. Click Continue in the User Account Control message box. A Connect To DNS Server dialog box appears.

16. Select the The Following Computer option and, in the text box, key **ServerDC**. Then, click OK. The DNS Manager console appears.

17. Expand the ServerDC node and the Forward Lookup Zones folder.

18. Right-click the contoso.com zone and, from the context menu, select New Alias (CNAME). The New Resource Record dialog box appears, as shown in Figure 5-2.

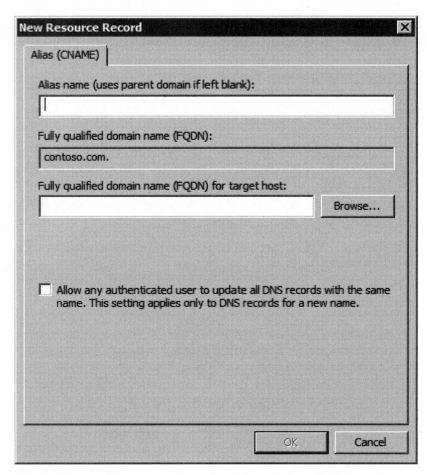

Figure 5-2
New Resource Record dialog box

19. In the Alias Name text box, key **www##**, where ## is the number assigned to your server.

20. In the Fully Qualified Domain Name (FQDN) For Target Host text box, key **server##.contoso.com**, where ## is the number assigned to your server. Then, click OK.

21. Repeat the process to create another New Alias (CNAME) record, using the alias name **sales##** and the target host name **server##.contoso.com**.

22. Press Ctrl+Prt Scr to take a screen shot of the DNS Manager console showing the two CNAME records you created. Pess Ctrl+V to paste the image on the page provided in the lab05_worksheet file.

23. Close the DNS Manager console, and leave the computer logged on for the next exercise.

Exercise 5.4	Creating Web Sites
Overview	To test IIS7's ability to support multiple Web sites simultaneously, create two new sites, and configure them to respond to different URLs.
Completion time	10 minutes

1. Open the Internet Information Services (IIS) Manager window, and expand the Sites node.

2. Right-click the Sites node and, from the context menu, select Add Web Site. The Add Web Site dialog box appears, as shown in Figure 5-3.

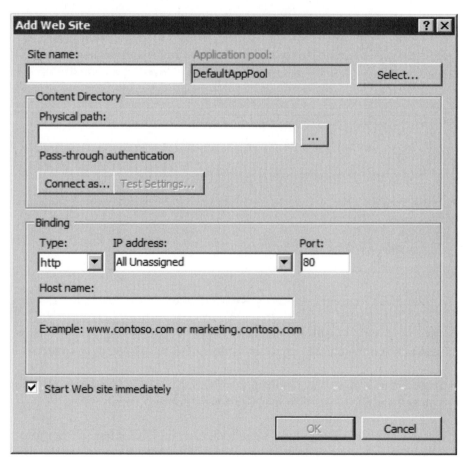

Figure 5-3
Add Web Site dialog box

3.   In the Site Name text box, key **www##**, where ## is the number assigned to your server.

4.   In the Physical Path text box, key or browse to the **\\ServerDC\Students\Student##\Documents\www##** folder.

5.   Click Connect As. The Connect As dialog box appears.

6.   Select the Specific User option, and click Set. The Set Credentials dialog box appears.

7.   In the User Name text box, key **contoso\Student##**, where ## is the number assigned to your server.

8.   In the Password and Confirm Password text boxes, key **P@ssw0rd**. Then, click OK.

9.   Click OK to close the Connect As dialog box.

Question 7	*Why is it necessary to supply credentials to access the directory you just created in the last exercise?*

10. In the Add Web Site dialog box, key **www##.contoso.com** in the Host Name text box, where ## is the number assigned to your server.

11. Click OK.

12. Create another Web site using the following settings:

   •   Site Name: sales##

   •   Physical Path: \\ServerDC\Students\Student##\Documents\sales##

   •   User Name: Student##

   •   Password: P@ssw0rd

   •   Host Name: sales##.contoso.com

13. Press Ctrl+Prt Scr to take a screen shot of the Internet Information Services (IIS) Manager window showing the two Web sites you created. Press Ctrl+V to paste the image on the page provided in the lab05_worksheet file.

14. In Internet Explorer, key **http://www##.contoso.com** in the address box, and press Enter.

Question 8	*What happens?*

15. Press Ctrl+Prt Scr to take a screen shot of the Internet Explorer window. Press Ctrl+V to paste the image on the page provided in the lab05_worksheet file.

16. Key **http://sales##.contoso.com** in the address box, and press Enter.

Question 9	*What happens now?*
Question 10	*How is IIS7 able to distinguish between the two URLs when the www## and sales## names resolve to the same IP address?*
Question 11	*Which Web page appears when you key the URL http://server##.contoso.com? Why?*
Question 12	*Which Web page appears when you key a URL containing the server's IP address instead of a name? Why?*

17. Leave the computer logged on for the next exercise.

Exercise 5.5   Creating Virtual Directories

Overview	In this exercise, use virtual directories to publish content found at a different location as part of an existing Web site.
Completion time	15 minutes

1. Open Windows Explorer, and browse to the Documents\www## folder you created in Exercise 5.3.

2. In the www## folder, create a subfolder called **Public**.

3. In the Public folder, use Notepad to create a file called **Default.htm** that contains the following text:

    ```
    <html><body>

    <h1><center>Contoso, Ltd.</center></h1>

    <h2><center>www##.contoso.com</center><h2>

    <h2><center>Public</center></h2>
    ```

4. In Internet Explorer, key **http://www##.contoso.com/public** in the address box, and press Enter. The Public page you created appears.

Question 13	*Why is the public folder you created accessible through the www## Web site?*

5. In the Internet Information Services (IIS) Manager window, right-click the www## site you created in Exercise 5.4 and, from the context menu, select Add Virtual Directory. The Add Virtual Directory dialog box appears, as shown in Figure 5-4.

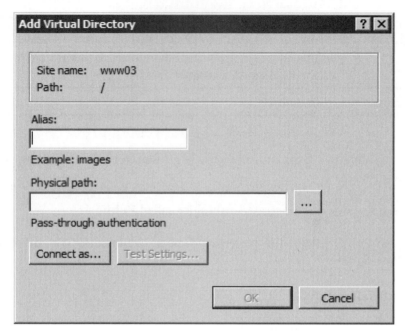

Figure 5-4
Add Virtual Directory dialog box

6. In the Alias text box, key **Links**.

7. In the Physical Path text box, key or browse to the **C:\Users\Student##\Links** folder, where ## is the number assigned to your computer.

8. Click Test Settings. The Test Connection dialog box appears.

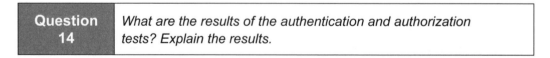

Question 14	*What are the results of the authentication and authorization tests? Explain the results.*

9. Click Close. The Test Connection dialog box closes.

10. In the Add Virtual Directory text box, click Connect As. The Connect As dialog box appears.

11. Select the Specific User option, and click Set. The Set Credentials dialog box appears.

12. In the User Name text box, key **contoso\Student##**, where ## is the number assigned to your server.

13. In the Password and Confirm Password text boxes, key **P@ssw0rd**. Then click OK.

14. Click OK to close the Connect As dialog box.

15. Click Test Settings again.

Question 15	*What are the results now?*
Question 16	*What URL must you use in Internet Explorer to access the virtual directory you just created?*

16. In Internet Explorer, key the URL for the Links virtual directory, and press Enter.

Question 17	*Why does an error page appear?*

17. In the Internet Information Services (IIS) Manager window, select the www## site. The *www## Home* Web page appears.

18. Double-click the Directory Browsing icon, and enable directory browsing.

19. Switch to Internet Explorer, and click the Refresh button.

Question 18	*What is the result?*

20. Create an identical Links virtual directory on your sales## site, and attempt to access it using Internet Explorer.

Question 19	*Why does the Links folder not appear?*

21. In the Internet Information Services (IIS) Manager window, with the www## site selected, click the Content View tab.

22. Press Ctrl+Prt Scr to take a screen shot of the Internet Information Services (IIS) Manager window. Press Ctrl+V to paste the image on the page provided in the lab05_worksheet file.

23. Close all open windows, and log off of the computer.

LAB REVIEW QUESTIONS

Completion time	5 minutes

1. In Exercise 5.2, you saw the two different types of error pages that IIS7 can generate. By default, the Web server displays detailed error pages in response to local requests and the simple error pages in response to remote requests. What is the main reason for providing less error information to remote users?

2. In Exercise 5.3, you created two CNAME resource records in your domain using the DNS Manager console. Why was it necessary to create these records?

3. In Exercise 5.3, why did you create CNAME resource records instead of standard Host (A) records in the DNS?

4. In Exercise 5.4, you configure your two new Web sites to use host name bindings. Why is this binding method preferable to using a different port number for each site?

LAB CHALLENGE: CREATING PORT NUMBER BINDINGS

Completion time	20 minutes

Your supervisor wants you to experiment with the different site binding strategies supported by IIS7. To complete this challenge, create a Web site called **testsite##**, containing the same type of dummy content you used earlier in this lab. The Web site must be accessible using any of the following URLs, where ## is replaced with the number assigned to your computer:

http://server##.contoso.com:1024

http://testsite##.contoso.com

http://testsite##.contoso.com:1025

http://testsite##.contoso##.com

http://testsite##.contoso##.com:1026

Create a list of the tasks you must perform to achieve your goal, and take five separate screen shots of the Internet Explorer window, displaying each of the five URLs successfully connected to the site. Paste the images in the lab05_worksheet file.

LAB 6
CONFIGURING IIS7

This lab contains the following exercises and activities:

BEFORE YOU BEGIN

The classroom network consists of Windows Server 2008 student servers and the ServerDC connected to a local area network. ServerDC, the domain controller for the contoso.com domain, is running Windows Server 2008. Throughout the labs in this manual, you will install, configure, maintain, and troubleshoot application roles, features, and services on the same student server.

To accommodate various types of classroom arrangements, each lab in this manual assumes that the student servers are in their baseline configuration, as described in Lab 1, "Preparing an Application Server." If you have not done so already, complete the initial configuration tasks in Exercise 1.1 of Lab 1 before beginning this lab.

Your instructor should have supplied the information needed to complete the following table:

Student computer name (Server##)	
Student account name (Student##)	

To complete the exercises in this lab, you must access a second student computer on the classroom network, referred to in the exercises as your *partner server*. Depending on the network configuration, use one of the following options, as directed by your instructor:

- For a conventional classroom network with one operating system installed on each computer, your lab partner must perform the same exercises on his or her computer, known as your partner server.

- For a classroom in which each computer uses local virtualization software to install multiple operating systems, you must perform the exercises separately on two virtual machines representing your student server and your partner server.

- For a classroom using online virtualization, you must perform the exercises separately on two virtual student servers, representing your student server and your partner server, in your Web browser.

Working with Lab Worksheets

Each lab in this manual requires that you answer questions, save images of your screen, or perform other activities that you document in a worksheet named for the lab, such as *lab06_worksheet*. Your instructor placed the worksheet files in the Students\Worksheets share on ServerDC. As you perform the exercises in each lab, open the appropriate worksheet file using WordPad, fill in the required information, and save the file to your computer's Student##\Documents folder. This folder is automatically redirected to the ServerDC computer. Your instructor will examine these worksheet files to assess your performance.

The procedure for opening and saving a worksheet file is as follows:

1. Click Start, and then click Run. The Run dialog box appears.

2. In the Open text box, key **\\ServerDC\Students\Worksheets\lab##_worksheet** (where lab## contains the number of the lab you're completing), and click OK. The worksheet document opens in WordPad.

3. Complete all of the exercises in the worksheet.

4. In WordPad, choose Save As from the File menu. The Save As dialog box appears.

5. In the File Name text box, key **lab##_worksheet_*yourname*** (where lab## contains the number of the lab you're completing, and *yourname* is your last name), and click Save.

SCENARIO

You are a new administrator for Contoso, Ltd., working on a test deployment of the application server technologies included with Windows Server 2008. In this lab, you test the security capabilities of the Web Server (IIS) role.

After completing this lab, you will be able to:

- Configure IP address restrictions

- Configure Web site authentication methods

- Secure a Web site with SSL

Estimated lab time: 80 minutes

Exercise 6.1	Installing the Web Server (IIS) Role
Overview	In this exercise, install IIS7 by adding the Web Server (IIS) role to the computer.
Completion time	5 minutes

1.   Turn on your computer. When the logon screen appears, log on using your *Student##* account and the password *P@ssw0rd*.

2.   Close the Initial Configuration Tasks window.

3.   Open Server Manager, and start the Add Roles Wizard.

4.   Click Next to bypass the *Before You Begin* page. The *Select Server Roles* page appears.

> **NOTE**
> *If your computer already has the Web Server (IIS) role installed with its default selection of role services, you can proceed immediately to Exercise 6.2. The sites and configuration settings you created in Lab 5 will not interfere with the completion of the Lab 6 exercises.*

5.   Select the Web Server (IIS) checkbox, and click Next. An Add Roles Wizard message box appears, listing the features required to add the Web Server (IIS) role.

6.   Click Add Required Features, and then click Next. The *Introduction To Web Server (IIS)* page appears.

7.   Click Next to bypass the introductory page. The *Select Role Services* page appears.

8. Click Next to accept the default role service selections. The *Confirm Installation Selections* page appears.

9. Click Install. The wizard installs the role.

10. Click Close.

11. Close Server Manager, and leave the computer logged on for the next exercise.

Exercise 6.2	Configuring IP Address Restrictions
Overview	In this exercise, you control access to a Web site based on the IP addresses of the client computers.
Completion time	15 minutes

1. Open Server Manager, and select the Roles node in the scope (left) pane.

2. In the detail (right) pane in the Web Server (IIS) section, click Add Role Services. The Add Role Services wizard appears, displaying the *Select Role Services* page.

3. Select the Security > IP and Domain Restrictions checkbox, and click Next. The *Confirm Installation Selections* page appears.

4. Click Install. The wizard installs the role service, and the *Installation Results* page appears.

5. Click Close.

6. Open Internet Explorer. In the address box, key **http://127.0.0.1**, and press Enter.

Question 1	*What happens?*

7. On your partner server, open Internet Explorer, and try to connect to the following URL: **http://server##.contoso.com**, where ## is the number assigned to your server (not your partner server).

Question 2	*What is the result?*
Question 3	*What can you infer from these results about the default settings of the IP and Domain Restrictions role service?*

8.   Open the Internet Information Services (IIS) Manager window, and expand the Server## and Sites nodes.

9.   Select Default Web Site. The *Default Web Site* home page appears.

10. Double-click the IPv4 Address and Domain Restrictions icon. The *IPv4 Address And Domain Restrictions* page appears, as shown in Figure 6-1.

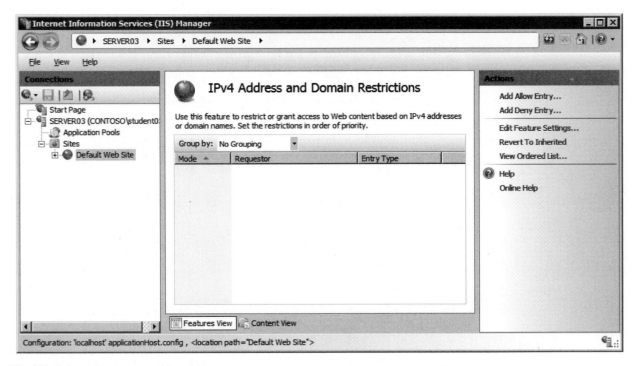

Figure 6-1
IPv4 Address And Domain Restrictions page

11. In the actions pane, click Edit Feature Settings. The Edit IP And Domain Restrictions Settings dialog box appears.

12. From the Access For Unspecified Clients drop-down list, select Deny, and click OK.

13. Switch to Internet Explorer, and click the Refresh button.

14. On your partner server, in Internet Explorer, try again to connect to http://server##.contoso.com.

15. In the Internet Information Services (IIS) Manager window, in the actions pane, click Add Allow Entry. The Add Allow Restriction Rule dialog box appears, as shown in Figure 6-2.

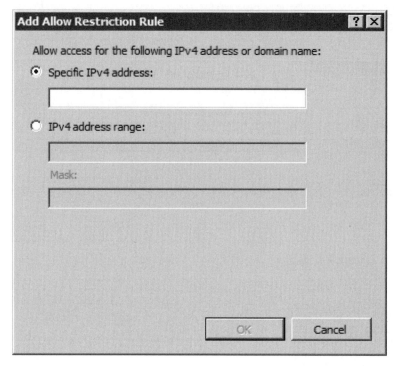

Figure 6-2
Add Allow Restriction Rule dialog box

16. Leave the Specific IPv4 Address option selected. In the text box, key **127.0.0.1**, and click OK. The new rule you created appears in the IPv4 Address And Domain Restrictions list.

17. Switch to Internet Explorer, and click the Refresh button.

Question 6	*What happens?*

18. On your partner server, switch to Internet Explorer, and try again to connect to the **http://server##.contoso.com** URL.

Question 7	*What is the result?*
Question 8	*Why can you connect to the Web site from one computer and not from the other?*

19. On your partner server, click Start. Then click All Programs > Accessories > Command Prompt. A command-prompt window appears.

20. In the command-prompt window, key **ipconfig**, and press Enter.

21. Key the computer name and IP address assigned to your partner server in the following table.

Computer Name	*IP Address*

22. Back on your own server, create a new Allow entry for your partner server's IP address.

23. Retest your access to the Web site from your server and your partner server, just as you did in steps 17 to 18.

Question 9	*What are the results?*
Question 10	*If you try connecting to your Web site from a network computer other than your server or your partner server, what would be the result? Why?*

24. In the Internet Information Services (IIS) Manager window, in the actions pane, click Add Allow Entry. The Add Allow Restriction Rule dialog box appears.

25. Select the IPv4 Address Range option and, in the text box, key **10.1.1.0**.

26. In the Mask text box, key **255.255.255.0**, and click OK. The new rule you created appears in the IPv4 Address And Domain Restrictions list.

27. Press Ctrl+Prt Scr to take a screen shot of the Internet Information Services (IIS) Manager window showing the three rules you created. Press Ctrl+V to paste the image on the page provided in the lab06_worksheet file.

28. Click Edit Feature Settings again, and select Allow from the Access For Unspecified Clients drop-down list. Then, click OK.

29. Leave the computer logged on for the next exercise.

Exercise 6.3	Configuring Anonymous Authentication
Overview	In this exercise, configure the properties of IIS7's Anonymous Authentication module.
Completion time	15 minutes

1. Open Server Manager, and select the Features node in the scope (left) pane.

> **NOTE**
>
> *If the Active Directory Domain Controller Tools feature was already installed in a previous lab, you can proceed directly to Step 6.*

2. In the detail (right) pane, click Add Features. The Add Features wizard appears, displaying the *Select Features* page.

3. Select the Remote Server Administration Tools > Active Directory Domain Services Tools > Active Directory Domain Controller Tools checkbox, and click Next. The *Confirm Installation Selections* page appears.

4. Click Install. The wizard installs the role service, and the *Installation Results* page appears.

5. Click Close.

6. Click Start. Then click Administrative Tools > Active Directory Users And Computers. The Active Directory Users And Computers console appears, as shown in Figure 6-3.

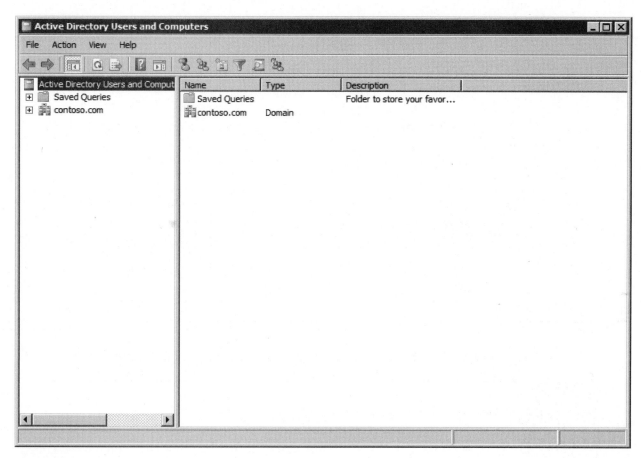

Figure 6-3
Active Directory Users And Computers console

7. In the Users container, create a new user account with the following properties:

   • First Name: IUSR##, where ## is the number assigned to your computer

   • User Logon Name: IUSR##

   • Password: P@ssw0rd

   • Clear the User Must Change Password At Next Logon checkbox

   • Select the Password Never Expires checkbox

8. Open the Properties sheet for the user account you just created, and click the Member Of tab.

9. Add the user to the IIS_IUSRS group, and click OK to close the Properties sheet.

NOTE

To review the steps for creating and managing domain user accounts, see Exercise 2.3 in Lab 2, "Deploying a File Server."

10. In the Internet Information Services (IIS) Manager window, select Default Web Site.

11. Double-click the Authentication icon. The *Authentication* page appears.

Question 11	*What authentication methods are provided in the default IIS7 configuration?*

12. In the list of authentication methods, select Anonymous Authentication. Then, in the actions pane, click Edit. The Edit Anonymous Authentication Credentials dialog box appears.

Question 12	*What anonymous user identity is IIS7 currently using?*

13. Click Set. The Set Credentials dialog box appears.

14. In the User Name text box, key **contoso\IUSR##**, where ## is the number assigned to your computer.

15. In the Password and Confirm Password text boxes, key **P@ssw0rd**.

16. Click OK to close the Set Credentials dialog box.

17. Click OK to close the Edit Anonymous Authentication Credentials dialog box.

18. In the Active Directory Users And Computers console, right-click the IUSR## object and, from the context menu, select Disable Account. An Active Directory Domain Services message box appears, informing you that the account is disabled.

19. Click OK.

20. Close all open windows, and restart the computer. Then, log on using your *Student##* account and the password *P@ssw0rd*.

21. Open Internet Explorer, and try to connect to the URL http://127.0.0.1.

Question 13	What happens? Explain your results.

22. Press Ctrl+Prt Scr to take a screen shot of the Internet Explorer window. Press Ctrl+V to paste the image on the page provided in the lab06_worksheet file.

23. Open the Active Directory Users And Computers console, right-click the IUSR## account you created and, on the context menu, click Enable Account.

24. Open the Internet Information Services (IIS) Manager window, select Default Web Site and, in the actions pane, click Restart.

25. Switch to Internet Explorer, and click the Refresh button.

Question 14	What happens? Explain your results.

26. Close Internet Explorer, and leave the computer logged on for the next exercise.

Exercise 6.4   Using Basic and Windows Authentication

Overview	In this exercise, install the Basic and Windows Authentication modules, and configure an IIS7 Web site to use them.
Completion time	10 minutes

1. Open Server Manager, and select the Roles node in the scope (left) pane.

2. In the detail (right) pane in the Web Server (IIS) section, click Add Role Services. The Add Role Services wizard appears, displaying the *Select Role Services* page.

3. Select the following role services, and click Next. The *Confirm Installation Selections* page appears.

   - Security > Basic Authentication

   - Security > Windows Authentication

   - Security > Digest Authentication

4. Click Install. The wizard installs the role service, and the *Installation Results* page appears.

5. Click Close.

6. In the Internet Information Services (IIS) Manager window, select Default Web Site, and double-click the Authentication icon. The *Authentication* home page appears, as shown in Figure 6-4.

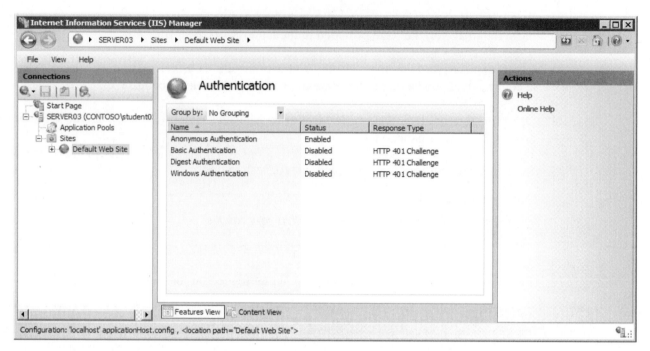

Figure 6-4
Authentication home page

Question 15	Which of the installed authentication modules is currently enabled?

7. Select Basic Authentication and, in the actions menu, select Enable.

8. Open Internet Explorer and, in the address box, key **http://server##.contoso.com**, where ## is the number assigned to your computer, and press Enter.

Question 16	What happens?
Question 17	Which authentication method is Internet Explorer currently using? How can you tell?

9.   In the Internet Information Services (IIS) Manager window, select Anonymous Authentication and, in the actions pane, select Disable.

10. Switch to Internet Explorer, and click the Refresh button.

Question 18	*What happens?*
Question 19	*Which authentication method is Internet Explorer using now? How can you tell?*

11. In the User Name text box, key **Student##**, where ## is the number of your computer. In the Password text box, key **P@ssw0rd**. Then click OK.

Question 20	*What happens?*

12. Try to log on two more times by entering the same credentials and clicking OK.

Question 21	*What happens after three failed logon attempts?*

13. Press Ctrl+Prt Scr to take a screen shot of the Internet Explorer window. Press Ctrl+V to paste the image on the page provided in the lab06_worksheet file.

14. In Internet Explorer, click the Refresh button, and try to log on with the user name *contoso\Student##* and the password *P@ssw0rd*.

Question 22	*What happens now?*

15. Close all Internet Explorer windows.

16. In the Internet Information Services (IIS) Manager window, select Windows Authentication and, in the actions pane, select Enable.

17. Open Internet Explorer, and connect again to http://server##.contoso.com, where ## is the number assigned to your computer.

18. Log on with the user name *contoso\Student##* and the password *P@ssw0rd*.

Question 23	What is the result?
Question 24	Which authentication method did Internet Explorer use to connect to the site? How can you tell?

19. Close all Internet Explorer windows.

20. In the Internet Information Services (IIS) Manager window, enable Anonymous Authentication, and disable Basic Authentication and Windows Authentication.

21. Leave the computer logged on for the next exercise.

Exercise 6.5   Configuring SSL

Overview	In this exercise, configure a Web site to use SSL encryption.
Completion time	10 minutes

1. In the Internet Information Services (IIS) Manager window, select your server node, and double-click the Server Certificates icon. The *Server Certificates* page appears, as shown in Figure 6-5.

Figure 6-5
Server Certificates page in the Internet Information Services (IIS) Manager window

2. In the actions pane, click Create Self-Signed Certificate. The Create Self-Signed Certificate dialog box appears.

3. In the Specify A Friendly Name For the Certificate text box, key **Server##**, where ## is the number assigned to your computer, and click OK. A new certificate appears in the Server Certificates list.

4. In the actions pane, click View. A Certificate dialog box appears.

5. Press Ctrl+Prt Scr to take a screen shot of the Certificate dialog box. Press Ctrl+V to paste the image on the page provided in the lab06_worksheet file.

6. Click OK to close the Certificate dialog box.

7. In the Internet Information Services (IIS) Manager window, select Default Web Site and, in the actions pane, click Bindings. The Site Bindings dialog box appears.

8. Click Add. The Add Site Binding dialog box appears.

9. In the Type dropdown list, select https.

10. In the SSL Certificate dropdown list, select Server##.

11. Click OK. The new binding appears in the Site Bindings dialog box.

Question 25	*Why are the two bindings listed in the Site Bindings box able to co-exist?*

12. Click Close to close the Site Bindings dialog box.

13. Double-click the SSL Settings icon. The *SSL Settings* page appears.

14. Select the Require SSL checkbox and the Require 128-bit SSL checkbox.

15. In the actions pane, click Apply. An information box appears, indicating that your changes have been saved.

16. Open an Internet Explorer window, and key **http://server##.contoso.com** in the address box, where ## is the number assigned to your computer. Then press Enter.

Question 26	*What happens?*

17. Press Ctrl+Prt Scr to take a screen shot of the Internet Explorer window. Press Ctrl+V to paste the image on the page provided in the lab06_worksheet file.

18. Key **https://server##.contoso.com** in the address box, and press Enter. (If a Security Alert message box appears, click OK to continue.)

Question 27	What happens now?

19. On your partner server, open an Internet Explorer window, and try to connect to your server using the same https://server##.contoso.com URL. A *Certificate Error* page appears.

Question 28	Why does the Web site fail to load from your partner server when it loaded successfully from your server?

20. Close the Internet Explorer window.

21. On your server, close all open windows, and log off.

LAB REVIEW QUESTIONS

Completion time	5 minutes

1. With the IP Address and Domain Restrictions settings configuration at the end of Exercise 6.2, would classroom computers other than your server and your partner server be able to access your Web site? Explain why or why not.

2. In Exercise 6.4, your repeated attempts to log on to your Web site using the *Student##* user name failed, but the logon was successful when you used the name *contoso\Student##*. Explain why.

3. In Exercise 6.4, why was it necessary to shut down Internet Explorer and then restart it before logging on with Windows Authentication?

LAB CHALLENGE: BUILDING A SECURE WEB SITE

Completion time	20 minutes

Your supervisor wants you create a test Web site, using all of the security mechanisms you tested. To complete this challenge, create a new Web site named SecureSite on your server. Make it accessible using the URL https://securesite.contoso.com. The site must adhere to the following requirements:

- The root directory must be accessible using Anonymous Authentication.

- Three subdirectories, called Tom, Dick, and Harry, must be accessible using only Basic Authentication.

- One virtual directory called Student##, pointing to the C:\Users\Student## folder, must be accessible using only Windows Authentication.

- The subdirectories and the virtual directory must be accessible only to users on the 10.1.1.0 network.

- The entire site must be secured using SSL with a self-signed certificate called SecureSite.

Take a screen shot of an Internet Explorer window showing the content of the Web site you created. Paste the image on the page provided in the lab06_worksheet file.

Take a screen shot of an Internet Explorer window showing the content of the virtual directory you created. Paste the image on the page provided in the lab06_worksheet file.

LAB 7
DEPLOYING AN
FTP SERVER

This lab contains the following exercises and activities:

BEFORE YOU BEGIN

The classroom network consists of Windows Server 2008 student servers and the ServerDC connected to a local area network. ServerDC, the domain controller for the contoso.com domain, is running Windows Server 2008. Throughout the labs in this manual, you will install, configure, maintain, and troubleshoot application roles, features, and services on the same student server.

To accommodate various types of classroom arrangements, each lab in this manual assumes that the student servers are in their baseline configuration, as described in Lab 1, "Preparing an Application Server." If you have not done so already, complete the initial configuration tasks in Exercise 1.1 of Lab 1 before beginning this lab.

Your instructor should have supplied the information needed to complete the following table:

Student computer name (Server##)	
Student account name (Student##)	

To complete the exercises in this lab, you must access a second student computer on the classroom network, referred to in the exercises as your *partner server*. Depending on the network configuration, use one of the following options, as directed by your instructor:

- For a conventional classroom network with one operating system installed on each computer, your lab partner must perform the same exercises on his or her computer, known as your partner server.

- For a classroom in which each computer uses local virtualization software to install multiple operating systems, you must perform the exercises separately on two virtual machines representing your student server and your partner server.

- For a classroom using online virtualization, you must perform the exercises separately on two virtual student servers, representing your student server and your partner server, in your Web browser.

Working with Lab Worksheets

Each lab in this manual requires that you answer questions, save images of your screen, or perform other activities that you document in a worksheet named for the lab, such as *lab07_worksheet*. Your instructor placed the worksheet files in the Students\Worksheets share on ServerDC. As you perform the exercises in each lab, open the appropriate worksheet file using WordPad, fill in the required information, and save the file to your computer's Student##\Documents folder. This folder is automatically redirected to the ServerDC computer. Your instructor will examine these worksheet files to assess your performance.

Use the following procedure to open and save a worksheet file.

1. Click Start, and then click Run. The Run dialog box appears.

2. In the Open text box, key **\\ServerDC\Students\Worksheets\lab##_worksheet** (where lab## contains the number of the lab you're completing), and click OK. The worksheet document opens in WordPad.

3. Complete all of the exercises in the worksheet.

4. In WordPad, choose Save As from the File menu. The Save As dialog box appears.

5. In the File Name text box, key **lab##_worksheet_*yourname*** (where lab## contains the number of the lab you're completing, and *yourname* is your last name), and click Save.

SCENARIO

You are a new administrator for Contoso, Ltd., working on a test deployment of the application server technologies included with Windows Server 2008. In this lab, you compare the capabilities of the FTP Publishing Service role service included with Windows Server 2008 and the Microsoft FTP Service for IIS 7.0 module, which is available as a free download.

After completing this lab, you will be able to:

- Create FTP sites

- Configure FTP security components

- Create FTP virtual directories

Estimated lab time: 95 minutes

Exercise 7.1	Installing the Web Server (IIS) Role
Overview	In this exercise, install IIS7 by adding the Web Server (IIS) role to the computer.
Completion time	5 minutes

1. Turn on your computer. When the logon screen appears, log on using your *Student##* account and the password *P@ssw0rd*.

2. Close the Initial Configuration Tasks window.

3. Open Server Manager, and start the Add Roles Wizard.

4. Click Next to bypass the *Before You Begin* page. The *Select Server Roles* page appears.

> **NOTE**
>
> *If your computer already has the Web Server (IIS) role installed with its default selection of role services, you can proceed immediately to Exercise 7.2. The sites and configuration settings you created in Labs 5 and 6 will not interfere with the completion of the Lab 7 exercises.*

5. Select the Web Server (IIS) checkbox, and click Next. An Add Roles Wizard message box appears, listing the features required to add the Web Server (IIS) role.

6. Click Add Required Features, and then click Next. The *Introduction to Web Server (IIS)* page appears.

7. Click Next to bypass the introductory page. The *Select Role Services* page appears.

8. Click Next to accept the default role service selections. The *Confirm Installation Selections* page appears.

9. Click Install. The wizard installs the role.

10. Click Close.

11. Close Server Manager, and leave the computer logged on for the next exercise.

Exercise 7.2	Creating an FTP6 Site
Overview	In this exercise, install the FTP Publishing Service role service, which provides basic FTP site hosting capabilities, and create a site.
Completion time	15 minutes

1. Open Server Manager, and select the Roles node in the scope (left) pane.

2. In the detail (right) pane in the Web Server (IIS) section, click Add Role Services. The Add Role Services Wizard appears, displaying the *Select Role Services* page.

3. Select the FTP Publishing Service checkbox. An Add Role Services Required For FTP Publishing Service dialog box appears, prompting you to install the IIS 6 Metabase Compatibility role service.

4. Click Add Required Role Services, and then click Next. The *Confirm Installation Selections* page appears.

5. Click Install. The wizard installs the role services, and the *Installation Results* page appears.

6. Click Close.

7. Click Start, and then click Administrative Tools > Internet Information Services (IIS) 6.0 Manager. After you click Continue in the User Account Control message box, the Internet Information Services (IIS) 6.0 Manager console appears.

8. Expand the Server## node and the FTP Sites folder, as shown in Figure 7-1.

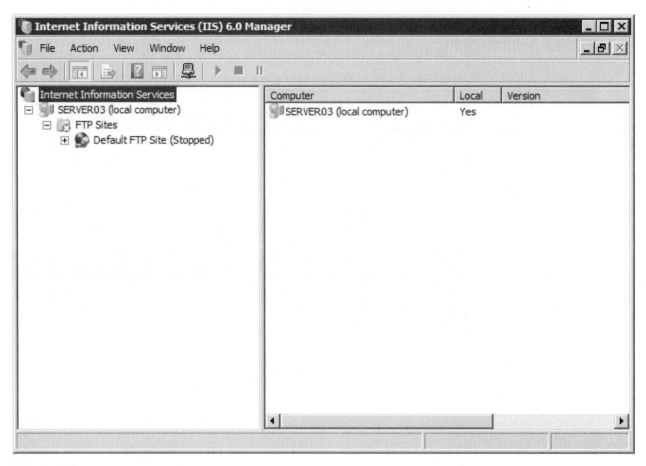

Figure 7-1
Internet Information Services (IIS) 6.0 Manager console

9. Right-click the FTP Sites folder and, from the context menu, select New > FTP Site. The FTP Site Creation Wizard appears.

10. Click Next to bypass the *Welcome* page. The *FTP Site Description* page appears.

11. In the description text box, key **FTP6-##,** where ## is the number assigned to your computer. Then click Next. The *IP Address And Port Settings* page appears.

12. Click Next to accept the default settings. The *FTP User Isolation* page appears.

Question 1	Why can an FTP site co-exist with the Default Web Site already installed on the server if neither one is using a unique host name?

13. Leave the Do Not Isolate Users option selected, and click Next. The *FTP Site Home Directory* page appears.

14. In the Path text box, key **C:\Users\Student##**, where ## is the number assigned to your computer, and click Next. The *FTP Site Access Permissions* page appears.

15. Select the Read and Write checkboxes, and click Next. A page appears, stating that the FTP Site Creation Wizard did not complete successfully.

16. Click Finish. The wizard creates the FTP site, but is unable to start it.

Question 2	Why was the wizard unable to start the new FTP site?

17. Right-click Default FTP Site and, from the context menu, select Start. The site is started.

18. Right-click Default FTP Site again and, from the context menu, select Stop. The site is stopped.

19. Right-click the FTP6-## site you just created and, from the context menu, select Start. The site starts.

NOTE	*In a newly installed FTP6 server, the default FTP appears to be stopped, but is not actually in a fully stopped state. Therefore, you must start it and stop it again before you can start the new FTP6-## site you created.*

20. Click Start, and then click All Programs > Accessories > Command Prompt. A command-prompt window appears.

21. In the command-prompt window, key **ftp server##.contoso.com**, where ## is the number assigned to your server, and press Enter.

22. When the User prompt appears, key **anonymous**, and press Enter.

23. When the Password prompt appears, press Enter.

Question 3	What happens?

24. Key **quit**, and press Enter.

25. Close the command-prompt window.

26. Open an Internet Explorer window, key **ftp://server##.contoso.com**, where ## is the number assigned to your server, and press Enter. An Internet Explorer dialog box appears, prompting you for logon credentials.

27. In the User Name text box, key **contoso\student##,** where ## is the number assigned to your server.

28. In the Password text box, key **P@ssw0rd**. Then click Log On.

Question 4	What happens now?

29. Press Ctrl+Prt Scr to take a screen shot of the Internet Explorer window. Press Ctrl+V to paste the image on the page provided in the lab07_worksheet file.

30. Leave the computer logged on for the next exercise.

Exercise 7.3	Configuring FTP6 Security
Overview	In this exercise, configure the security properties available to FTP6 sites.
Completion time	10 minutes

1. In the Internet Information Services (IIS) 6.0 Manager console, right-click the FTP6-## site you created in Exercise 7.2 and, on the context menu, select Properties. The FTP6-## Properties sheet appears, like the sample shown in Figure 7-2.

Figure 7-2
FTP6-03 Properties sheet

2.   Click the Security Accounts tab.

> **Question 5**   *What user account does FTP6 use for anonymous connections by default?*

3.   Leave the Allow Anonymous Connections checkbox selected and, in the User Name text box, key **contoso\Student##,** where ## is the number assigned to your computer.

4.   In the Password text box, key **P@ssw0rd**, and click Apply. A Confirm Password dialog box appears.

5.   Re-enter the password for confirmation, and click OK.

6.   Press Ctrl+Prt Scr to take a screen shot of the Security Accounts tab of the Properties sheet. Press Ctrl+V to paste the image on the page provided in the lab07_worksheet file.

7.   Click the Home Directory tab.

8.   Clear the Write checkbox.

9.   Click the Directory Security tab.

10.   Select the Denied Access option, and then click Add. The Grant Access dialog box appears.

11.   Select the Group Of Computers option.

12.   In the IP Address text box, key **10.1.1.0**.

13.   In the Subnet Mask text box, key **255.255.255.0**.

14.   Press Ctrl+Prt Scr to take a screen shot of the Directory Security tab of the Properties sheet. Press Ctrl+V to paste the image on the page provided in the lab07_worksheet file.

15.   Click OK twice to close the Grant Access dialog box and the Properties sheet.

16.   On your partner server, open a command-prompt window, and try to connect to your computer by keying **ftp server##.contoso.com**, where ## is the number assigned to your computer.

17.   When the User prompt appears, key **anonymous**, and press Enter.

18. When the Password prompt appears, press Enter.

Question 6	What is the result?

19. Close the Command Prompt window on your partner server, and leave the computer logged on for the next exercise.

Exercise 7.4	Installing FTP7
Overview	In this exercise, install the FTP7 module your instructor made available on the classroom server. However, before you can install the FTP7, you must remove the role services you added to support FTP6.
Completion time	10 minutes

1. Open Server Manager, and select the Roles node.

2. In the Web Server (IIS) role section, click Remove Role Services. The Remove Role Services Wizard appears, displaying the *Select Role Services* page.

3. Clear the following checkboxes, and click Next. The *Confirm Removal Selections* page appears.

   - FTP Publishing Service

   - IIS 6 Metabase Compatibility

4. Click Remove. The wizard removes the role services.

5. Click Close. A Remove Role Services message box appears, prompting you to restart the computer.

6. Click Yes. The computer restarts.

7. When the logon screen appears, log on using your *Student##* account and the password *P@ssw0rd*.

8. The Server Manager console reloads and completes the role service removal process.

9. Click Close. The wizard closes.

10. Open Windows Explorer, and browse to the \\ServerDC\Install\FTP7 folder.

11. Double-click the ftp7_x86_rtw.msi file. An Open File – Security Warning message box appears, asking whether you want to run the file.

12. Click Run. The Microsoft FTP Service for IIS 7.0 Setup Wizard appears, displaying the *Welcome* page.

13. Click Next. The *End-User License Agreement* page appears.

14. Select the I Accept The Terms In The License Agreement checkbox, and click Next. The *Custom Setup* page appears, as shown in Figure 7-3.

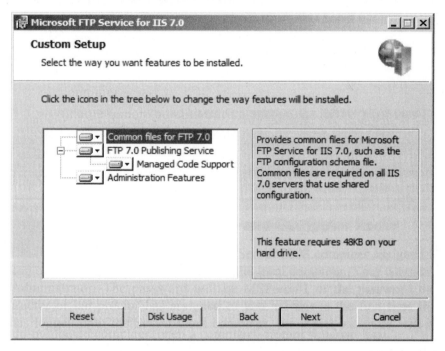

Figure 7-3
Custom Setup page of the Microsoft FTP Service for IIS 7.0 Setup Wizard

15. Click Next to accept the default selections. The *Ready To Install* page appears.

16. Click Install. Click Continue in the User Account Control message box to continue the installation. The *Completed The Setup Wizard* page appears.

17. Press Ctrl+Prt Scr to take a screen shot of the *Completed The Setup Wizard* page. Press Ctrl+V to paste the image on the page provided in the lab07_worksheet file.

18. Click Finish.

19. Leave the computer logged on for the next exercise.

Exercise 7.5	Creating an FTP7 Site
Overview	In this exercise, create a site using FTP7, and test its connectivity.
Completion time	10 minutes

1. Open the Internet Information Services (IIS) Manager window, and expand the server node, as shown in Figure 7-4.

Figure 7-4
Internet Information Services (IIS) Manager window

Question 7	*What difference between FTP6 and FTP7 is already evident?*

2. Right-click the Sites node and, from the context menu, select Add FTP Site. The Add FTP Site Wizard appears, displaying the *Site Information* page.

3. In the FTP Site Name text box, key **FTP7-##,** where ## is the number assigned to your computer.

4. In the Physical Path text box, key or browse to the **C:\Inetpub\wwwroot** folder.

5. Click Next. The *Binding And SSL Settings* page appears.

6. In the SSL box, select the Allow SSL option, and click Next. The *Authentication And Authorization Information* page appears.

7. In the Authentication box, select the Anonymous checkbox.

8. In the Authorization box, select All Users from the Allow Access To drop-down list.

9. Under Permissions, select the Read and Write checkboxes.

10. Click Finish. The new site appears.

11. Open Internet Explorer, key **ftp://server##.contoso.com** in the address box, where ## is the number assigned to your computer, and press Enter.

Question 8	What happens?

12. Press Ctrl+Prt Scr to take a screen shot of the Internet Explorer window. Press Ctrl+V to paste the image on the page provided in the lab07_worksheet file.

13. On your partner server, open Internet Explorer, and use the same URL to connect to the FTP site on your server.

Question 9	Why are you unable to connect to your FTP site from your partner server?

14. On your server, click Start, and then click Control Panel. The Control Panel window appears.

15. Double-click the Windows Firewall icon. The Windows Firewall window appears.

16. Click Change Settings. Click Continue in the User Account Control message box to display the Windows Firewall Settings dialog box, as shown in Figure 7-5.

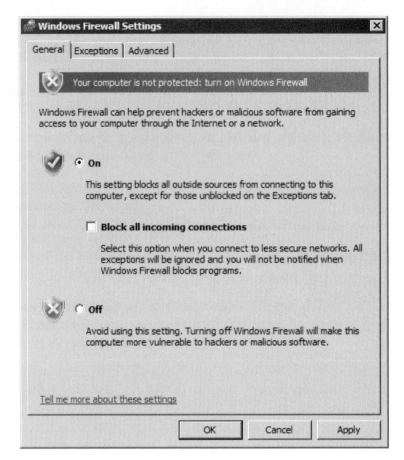

Figure 7-5
Windows Firewall Settings dialog box

17. Click the Off option, and then click OK.

> **NOTE**
> *In the classroom environment, you can safely disable Windows Firewall without endangering your server. However, on an actual FTP server, you must leave your firewall active and configure it to permit FTP traffic to pass.*

18. Return to your partner server, and try again to connect to the FTP site on your server.

Question 10	*What happens?*

19. Leave the Internet Information Services (IIS) Manager window open for the next exercise.

Exercise 7.6   Creating an FTP7 Virtual Directory

Overview	In this exercise, create a virtual directory on your FTP site.
Completion time	10 minutes

1. In the Internet Information Services (IIS) Manager window, right-click the FTP7-## site and, from the context menu, select Add Virtual Directory. The Add Virtual Directory dialog box appears, as shown in Figure 7-6.

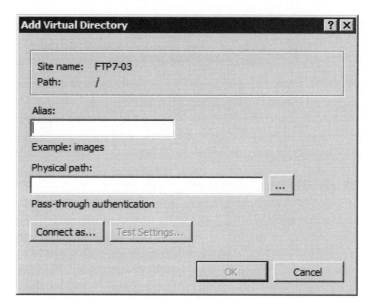

Figure 7-6
Add Virtual Directory dialog box

2. In the Alias text box, key **Student##**, where ## is the number assigned to your computer.

3. In the Physical Path text box, key or browse to the **C:\Users\Student##** folder.

4. Click Connect As. The Connect As dialog box appears.

5. Select the Specific User option, and click Set. The Set Credentials dialog box appears.

6. In the User Name text box, key **contoso\student##,** where ## is the number assigned to your computer.

7. In the Password and Confirm Password text boxes, key **P@ssw0rd**, and click OK.

8. Click OK to close the Connect As dialog box.

9. Click OK to close the Add Virtual Directory dialog box.

10. Open Internet Explorer, key **ftp://server##.contoso.com** in the address box, where ## is the number assigned to your computer, and press Enter.

Question 11	What happens?

11. In Internet Explorer, key **ftp://server##.contoso.com/student##** in the address box, where ## in both places is the number assigned to your computer, and then press Enter.

Question 12	What happens now?

12. Press Ctrl+Prt Scr to take a screen shot of the Internet Explorer window containing the contents of the student## folder. Press Ctrl+V to paste the image on the page provided in the lab07_worksheet file.

13. Close all open windows, and log off.

LAB REVIEW QUESTIONS

Completion time	5 minutes

1. In Exercise 7.3, after you configure the FTP6 security options, why is it unnecessary for you to log on to connect to the FTP site on your server?

2. In Exercise 7.6, you added a virtual directory to your FTP7 site and displayed the contents of the virtual directory in Internet Explorer. However, when you first connected to the FTP site, the virtual directory did not appear in the site listing. To complete this exercise, configure IIS7 to display the virtual directory as part of the FTP site's directory listing. Explain the changes you made, and take a screen shot of the Internet Explorer window containing the virtual directory name. Paste the image in the lab07_worksheet file.

LAB CHALLENGE: CREATING A COMBINED WEB/FTP SITE

Completion time	20 minutes

Your supervisor wants you to create a combined Web/FTP solution that enables a specific user to access his or her user profile folder on your server. To complete this challenge, create a site that provides both HTTP and FTP access to your Student## account's user profile folder (C:\Users\Student##), subject to the following restrictions:

- The HTTP and FTP sites must be accessible using the URLs

    http://student##.contoso.com and ftp://student##.contoso.com, respectively.

- HTTP access must use Windows Authentication.

- FTP access must use Basic Authentication.

- The site must be accessible only by the Student## user.

- The user must be able to see a directory listing, whether connected using HTTP or FTP.

List the tasks you must complete to create and configure the site, and then take two screen shots of the Internet Explorer window showing the HTTP and FTP connections. Paste the image on the page provided in the lab07_worksheet file.

WORKSTATION RESET: RETURN TO BASELINE

Completion time	10 minutes

After this lab, you will not need the Web Server (IIS) role installed in your server until later in the manual. To return the computer to its baseline state, complete the following procedures.

1. Open the Internet Information Services (IIS) Manager window, and delete the FTP sites, Web sites, and virtual directory you created during the lab.

2. Open the Server Manager console, and remove the Web Server (IIS) role, as well as any features you added during the lab.

3. Open the Windows Firewall control panel, and turn on the firewall.

> **NOTE**
>
> *Depending on the configuration of your classroom network, it might not be necessary to complete the workstation reset. Check with your instructor before you complete this procedure.*

LAB 8
DEPLOYING A TERMINAL SERVER

This lab contains the following exercises and activities:

Exercise 8.1	Installing the Terminal Services Role
Exercise 8.2	Using the Remote Desktop Connection Client
Exercise 8.3	Creating an RDP File
Exercise 8.4	Remotely Configuring RDC Client Settings
Lab Review	Questions
Lab Challenge	Automating a Terminal Server Connection
Workstation Reset	Return to Baseline

BEFORE YOU BEGIN

The classroom network consists of Windows Server 2008 student servers and the ServerDC connected to a local area network. ServerDC, the domain controller for the Contoso.com domain, is running Windows Server 2008. Throughout the labs in this manual, you will install, configure, maintain, and troubleshoot application roles, features, and services on the same student server.

To accommodate various types of classroom arrangements, each lab in this manual assumes that the student servers are in their baseline configuration, as described in Lab 1, "Preparing an Application Server." If you have not done so already, complete the initial configuration tasks in Exercise 1.1 of Lab 1 before beginning this lab.

Your instructor should have supplied the information needed to complete the following table:

Student computer name (Server##)	
Student account name (Student##)	

To complete the exercises in this lab, you must access a second student computer on the classroom network, referred to in the exercises as your *partner server*. Depending on the network configuration, use one of the following options, as directed by your instructor:

- For a conventional classroom network with one operating system installed on each computer, your lab partner must perform the same exercises on his or her computer, known as your partner server.

- For a classroom in which each computer uses local virtualization software to install multiple operating systems, you must perform the exercises separately on two virtual machines representing your student server and your partner server.

- For a classroom using online virtualization, you must perform the exercises separately on two virtual student servers, representing your student server and your partner server, in your Web browser.

Working with Lab Worksheets

Each lab in this manual requires that you answer questions, save images of your screen, or perform other activities that you document in a worksheet named for the lab, such as *lab08_worksheet*. Your instructor placed the worksheet files in the Students\Worksheets share on ServerDC. As you perform the exercises in each lab, open the appropriate worksheet file using WordPad, fill in the required information, and save the file to your computer's Student##\Documents folder. This folder is automatically redirected to the ServerDC computer. Your instructor will examine these worksheet files to assess your performance.

Use the following procedure to open and save a worksheet file.

1. Click Start, and then click Run. The Run dialog box appears.

2. In the Open text box, key **\\ServerDC\Students\Worksheets\lab##_worksheet** (where lab## contains the number of the lab you're completing), and click OK. The worksheet document opens in WordPad.

3. Complete all of the exercises in the worksheet.

4. In WordPad, choose Save As from the File menu. The Save As dialog box appears.

5. In the File Name text box, key **lab##_worksheet_*yourname*** (where lab## contains the number of the lab you're completing, and *yourname* is your last name), and click Save.

SCENARIO

You are a new administrator for Contoso, Ltd., working on a test deployment of the application server technologies included with Windows Server 2008. In this lab, you begin exploring the capabilities of the Terminal Services role included with Windows Server 2008.

After completing this lab, you will be able to:

- Install the Terminal Services role

- Configure the Remote Desktop Connection client

- Create an RDP file

- Configure Terminal Server configuration settings

Estimated lab time: 80 minutes

Exercise 8.1	Installing the Terminal Services Role
Overview	For Windows Server 2008 to function as a terminal server, you must install the Terminal Services role. In this exercise, you add the role with the Terminal Server role service, enabling the server to provide basic Terminal Services functionality.
Completion time	10 minutes

1. Turn on your computer. When the logon screen appears, log on using your *Student##* account and the password *P@ssw0rd*.

2. Close the Initial Configuration Tasks window.

3. Open Server Manager, and start the Add Roles Wizard.

4. Click Next to bypass the *Before You Begin* page. The *Select Server Roles* page appears.

> **NOTE**
> *If your computer has any other roles or features installed, remove them before you proceed with this lab.*

5. Select the Terminal Services checkbox, as shown in Figure 8-1, and click Next. The *Introduction To Terminal Services* page appears.

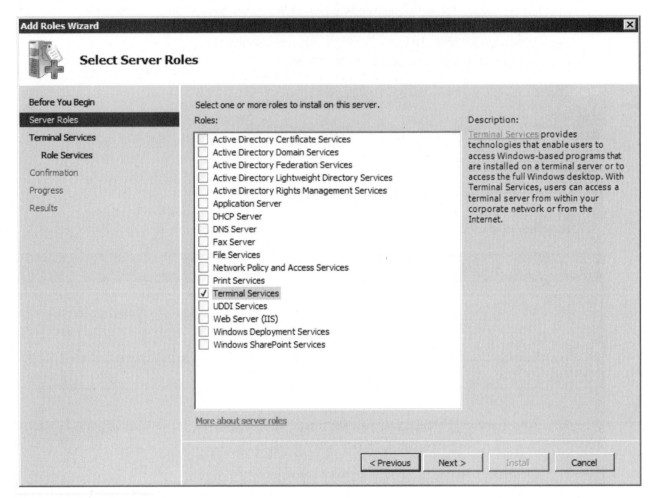

Figure 8-1
Select Server Roles page of the Add Roles Wizard

6. Click Next to bypass the introductory page. The *Select Role Services* page appears.

7. Select the Terminal Server role service, and click Next. The *Uninstall And Reinstall Applications For Compatibility* page appears.

8. Click Next to continue. The *Specify Authentication Method For Terminal Server* page appears.

9. Select the Do Not Require Network Level Authentication option, and click Next. The *Specify Licensing Mode* page appears.

10. Select the Configure Later option, and click Next. The *Select User Groups Allowed To Access This Terminal Server* page appears.

11. Click Add. The Select Users, Computers, Or Groups dialog box appears.

12. In the Enter Object Names To Select box, key **Students**, and click OK.

13. Press Ctrl+Prt Scr to take a screen shot of the *Select User Groups Allowed To Access This Terminal Server* page. Press Ctrl+V to paste the image on the page provided in the lab08_worksheet file.

14. Click Next to accept the specified groups. The *Confirm Installation Selections* page appears.

15. Click Install. The wizard installs the role.

16. Click Close. An Add Roles Wizard message box appears, prompting you to restart the computer.

17. Click Yes. The computer restarts.

18. When the logon screen appears, log on using your *Student##* account and the password *P@ssw0rd.* Server Manager loads and completes the role installation.

19. Click Close.

20. Close Server Manager, and leave the computer logged on for the next exercise.

Exercise 8.2	Using the Remote Desktop Connection Client
Overview	In this exercise, initiate a Terminal Services connection to your partner server using the Remote Desktop Connection client.
Completion time	15 minutes

1. Click Start, and then click All Programs > Accessories > Notepad. A Notepad window appears.

2. Key some text in the Notepad window, and then click File > Save As. The Save As combo box appears.

3. Save the text file to your Documents folder using the name **Lab08**.

4. Close the Notepad window.

5. Click Start, and then click All Programs > Accessories > Remote Desktop Connection. The Remote Desktop Connection dialog box appears.

6.   Click Options. The dialog box expands, as shown in Figure 8-2.

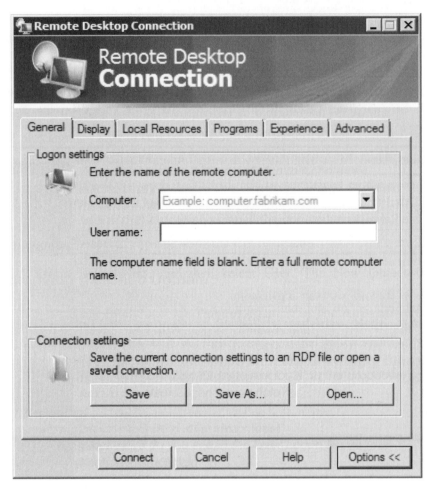

Figure 8-2
Remote Desktop Connection dialog box

7.   Click the Display tab.

8.   In the Remote Desktop Size box, use the slider to select a lower resolution for your current display.

9.   Click the Local Resources tab.

10. In the Remote Computer Sound box, select Do Not Play from the drop-down list.

11. In the Local Devices And Resources box, clear the Printers checkbox, and leave the Clipboard checkbox selected.

12. Click the Experience tab.

13. In the Performance drop-down list, select LAN (10 Mbps Or Higher).

14. Click the General tab.

15. In the Computer text box, key **Server##,** where ## is the number assigned to your partner server.

16. In the User Name field, key **contoso\student##,** where ## is the number assigned to your computer.

> **NOTE**
>
> *Before you initiate the connection to your partner server, verify that Exercise 8.1 has been completed on that computer and is ready to receive remote connections.*

17. Click Connect. A Windows Security dialog box appears.

18. Under the contoso\student## user name, key **P@ssw0rd**, and click OK. A Server## - Remote Desktop window appears.

19. Close any windows that appear.

20. In the Server## - Remote Desktop window, click Start, and then click All Programs > Accessories > Notepad. A Notepad window appears.

Question 1	*Which computer is running Notepad?*

21. Click File > Open. The Open combo box appears.

22. Press Ctrl+Prt Scr to take a screen shot of the Server## - Remote Desktop window showing the Open combo box. Press Ctrl+V to paste the image on the page provided in the lab08_worksheet file.

Question 2	*Which computer is storing the user profile that appears within the Student## folder, where ## is the number assigned to your computer?*

23. Select the Lab08 text file you created at the beginning of this exercise, and click Open.

24. Modify the text, and save the file.

25. Leave the Notepad window open, and click the Close button in the title bar of the Server## - Remote Desktop window. A Disconnect Terminal Services Session message box appears, asking whether you want to disconnect.

26. Click OK. The RDC client disconnects from the terminal server.

Question 3	*Is Notepad still running on your partner server? Explain why or why not.*

27. Leave the computer logged on for the next exercise.

Exercise 8.3	Creating an RDP File
Overview	In this exercise, use the RDC client to create an RDP file, which you can use to connect to a specific terminal server using a predetermined collection of configuration settings.
Completion time	10 minutes

1. Click Start, and then click All Programs > Accessories > Remote Desktop Connection. The Remote Desktop Connection dialog box appears.

2. Click Options. The dialog box expands.

3. In the Connection Settings box, click Save As. The Save As combo box appears.

4. Click Browse Folders. The combo box expands, as shown in Figure 8-3.

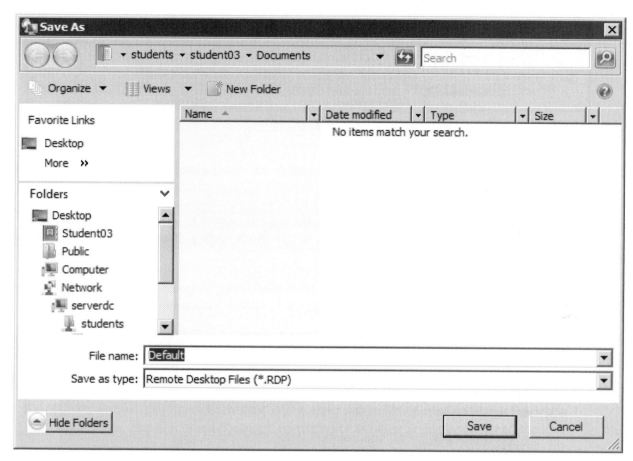

Figure 8-3
Save As combo box

5.   In the left pane, click Desktop.

6.   In the File Name text box, key **Server##,** where ## is the number assigned to your partner server.

7.   Click Save. A Server## icon appears on your desktop.

8.   Click the Display tab.

9.   In the Remote Desktop Size box, set the slider to Full Screen.

10. Click Connect. A Remote Desktop Connection message box appears, asking whether you trust the remote connection.

11. Click Connect. The Windows Security dialog box appears.

12. Log on using the password *P@ssw0rd*, and click OK. The RDC client connects to the terminal server and the desktop appears, with the Notepad window you opened in Exercise 8.2 still open.

Question 4	Is the taskbar at the bottom of your screen generated by your server or your partner server? How can you tell?

13. Click the Close button in the connection bar to disconnect from the terminal server session.

14. Press Ctrl+Prt Scr to take a screen shot of your server's desktop showing the Server## RDP icon. Press Ctrl+V to paste the image on the page provided in the lab08_worksheet file.

15. Double-click the Server## icon. A Remote Desktop Connection message box appears, warning you that the publisher of the remote connection cannot be identified.

16. Click Connect. Log on using the password *P@ssw0rd*, and click OK. The RDC client connects to the terminal server.

17. In the remote session window, click Start. Then click the arrow button and, on the context menu, click Log Off.

Question 5	What happens?
Question 6	Is the Notepad window you opened in Exercise 8.2 still open in the terminal server session? Why or why not?

18. Leave the computer logged on for the next exercise.

Exercise 8.4	Remotely Configuring RDC Client Settings
Overview	In this exercise, use the Terminal Services Configuration console to set parameters that control the behavior of RDC clients when they connect to that server.
Completion time	15 minutes

1. Click Start, and then click Administrative Tools > Terminal Services > Terminal Services Configuration. Click Continue on the User Account Control message box to display the Terminal Services Configuration console shown in Figure 8-4.

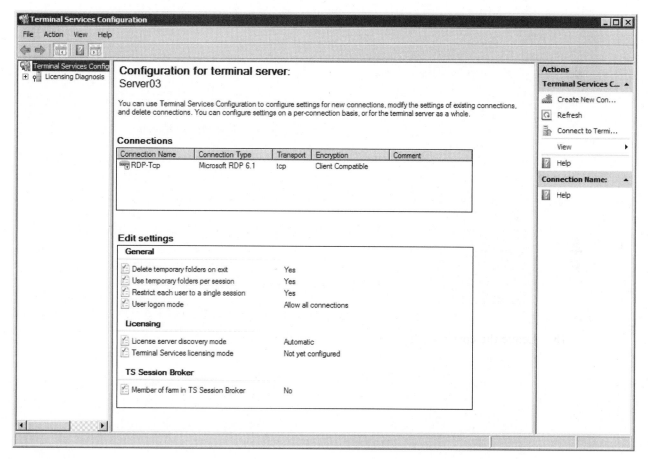

Figure 8-4
Terminal Services Configuration console

2. In the Connections box, right-click the RDP-Tcp connection and, on the context menu, click Properties. The RDP-Tcp Properties sheet appears.

3. Click the Environment tab.

4. Select the Start The Following Program When The User Logs On option.

5. In the Program Path And File Name text box, key **C:\Windows\System32\Notepad.exe**. In the Start In text box, key **c:\users\%username%**.

6. Press Ctrl+Prt Scr to take a screen shot of the Environment tab on the RDP-Tcp Properties sheet. Press Ctrl+V to paste the image on the page provided in the lab08_worksheet file.

7. Click OK. A Terminal Services Configuration message box appears, informing you that changes have been made to the system registry.

8. Click OK.

> **NOTE**
>
> *Before you continue, verify that steps 1–8 have been completed on your partner server.*

9. Open the Remote Desktop Connection dialog box, and click Options.

10. Click the Programs tab.

11. Select the Start The Following Program On Connection checkbox.

12. In the Program Path And File Name text box, key **C:\Windows\System32\Calc.exe**.

13. Press Ctrl+Prt Scr to take a screen shot of the Programs tab on the RDP-Tcp Properties sheet. Press Ctrl+V to paste the image on the page provided in the lab08_worksheet file.

14. Click Connect. Log on using the password *P@ssw0rd*, and click OK. The RDC client connects to the terminal server.

Question 7	*Which program loads automatically after the RDC client establishes a session with the terminal server?*
Question 8	*Based on these results, what can you determine about the relationship between the configuration settings in the RDC client and those in the Terminal Services Configuration console?*
Question 9	*How does this Terminal Services session differ from the sessions in the previous exercises?*

15. In the Notepad window, click File > Exit.

Question 10	*What happens?*

16. In the Terminal Services Configuration console, open the RDP-Tcp Properties sheet. Restore the original settings on the Environment tab by selecting the Run Initial Program Specified By User Profile And Remote Desktop Connection Or Client option.

17. Open the Remote Desktop Connection dialog box and, on the Programs tab, clear the Start The Following Program On Connection checkbox.

18. Start the connection process to apply the configuration changes, and then cancel the connection.

19. Close all open windows, and log off of the computer.

LAB REVIEW QUESTIONS

Completion time	5 minutes

1. In Exercise 8.1, after you finish installing the Terminal Server role service, a bubble message warns you that Terminal Services Licensing is not configured on the server and Terminal Services will stop working after 120 days. What must you do to keep Terminal Services working beyond the 120-day grace period?

2. In Exercise 8.2, you created a Lab08 text file on your computer at the beginning of the exercise. Later, while working within a terminal server session on your partner server, you opened a file using Notepad and accessed the Documents folder in your user profile on the partner server. Why is the Lab08 file displayed in the Documents folder on your partner server when you originally created it on your own server?

3. In Exercise 8.3, you used the RDC client to connect to your partner server twice: one connection was made interactively, and one connection used the RDP file you created. From this experience, how can you tell whether the RDP file includes the settings you configured in the client before creating the RDP file?

LAB CHALLENGE: AUTOMATING A TERMINAL SERVER CONNECTION

Completion time	15 minutes

Your supervisor wants you to create a batch file/logon script that will automatically connect a workstation to a Windows Server 2008 terminal server farm called HOME01 in full screen mode. To complete this challenge, create the necessary files, and store them in your Student##/Documents folder.

WORKSTATION RESET: RETURN TO BASELINE

Completion time	10 minutes

To accommodate the various classroom configurations supported by this manual, each lab concludes with the student computer returned to the baseline state noted at the end of Exercise 1.1 in Lab 1, "Preparing an Application Server." To return the computer to this state, complete the following procedures.

1. Open the Server Manager console, and remove the Terminal Services role, as well as any features you added during the lab.

> **NOTE**
> *Depending on the configuration of your classroom network, it might not be necessary to complete the workstation reset. Check with your instructor before you complete this procedure.*

LAB 9
USING REMOTEAPP

This lab contains the following exercises and activities:

BEFORE YOU BEGIN

The classroom network consists of Windows Server 2008 student servers and the ServerDC connected to a local area network. ServerDC, the domain controller for the contoso.com domain, is running Windows Server 2008. Throughout the labs in this manual, you will install, configure, maintain, and troubleshoot application roles, features, and services on the same student server.

To accommodate various types of classroom arrangements, each lab in this manual assumes that the student servers are in their baseline configuration, as described in Lab 1, "Preparing an Application Server." If you have not done so already, complete the initial configuration tasks in Exercise 1.1 of Lab 1 before beginning this lab.

Your instructor should have supplied the information needed to complete the following table:

Student computer name (Server##)	
Student account name (Student##)	

To complete the exercises in this lab, you must access a second student computer on the classroom network, referred to in the exercises as your *partner server*. Depending on the network configuration, use one of the following options, as directed by your instructor:

- For a conventional classroom network with one operating system installed on each computer, your lab partner must perform the same exercises on his or her computer, known as your partner server.

- For a classroom in which each computer uses local virtualization software to install multiple operating systems, you must perform the exercises separately on two virtual machines representing your student server and your partner server.

- For a classroom using online virtualization, you must perform the exercises separately on two virtual student servers, representing your student server and your partner server, in your Web browser.

Working with Lab Worksheets

Each lab in this manual requires that you answer questions, save images of your screen, or perform other activities that you document in a worksheet named for the lab, such as *lab09_worksheet*. Your instructor placed the worksheet files in the Students\Worksheets share on ServerDC. As you perform the exercises in each lab, open the appropriate worksheet file using WordPad, fill in the required information, and save the file to your computer's Student##\Documents folder. This folder is automatically redirected to the ServerDC computer. Your instructor will examine these worksheet files to assess your performance.

Use the following procedure to open and save a worksheet file.

1. Click Start, and then click Run. The Run dialog box appears.

2. In the Open text box, key **\\ServerDC\Students\Worksheets\lab##_worksheet** (where lab## contains the number of the lab you're completing), and click OK. The worksheet document opens in WordPad.

3. Complete all of the exercises in the worksheet.

4. In WordPad, choose Save As from the File menu. The Save As dialog box appears.

5. In the File Name text box, key **lab##_worksheet_*yourname*** (where lab## contains the number of the lab you're completing, and *yourname* is your last name), and click Save.

SCENARIO

You are a new administrator for Contoso, Ltd., working on a test deployment of the application server technologies included with Windows Server 2008. In this lab, you explore the capabilities of the new RemoteApp features in Windows Server 2008 Terminal Services.

After completing this lab, you will be able to:

- Install the Terminal Services role

- Configure RemoteApp to deploy specific applications

- Create RemoteApp RDP and MSI files

- Use Terminal Server Manager to monitor Terminal Services activities

Estimated lab time: 70 minutes

Exercise 9.1	Installing the Terminal Services Role
Overview	For Windows Server 2008 to function as a terminal server, you first must install the Terminal Services role. In this exercise, add the role with the Terminal Server role service, enabling the server to provide basic Terminal Services functionality.
Completion time	10 minutes

1. Turn on your computer. When the logon screen appears, log on using your *Student##* account and the password *P@ssw0rd*.

2. Close the Initial Configuration Tasks window.

3. Open Server Manager, and start the Add Roles Wizard.

4. Click Next to bypass the *Before You Begin* page. The *Select Server Roles* page appears.

> **NOTE** *If your computer has the Terminal Services role installed with its default selection of role services, you can proceed immediately to Exercise 9.2.*

5. Select the Terminal Services checkbox, and click Next. The *Introduction To Terminal Services* page appears.

6. Click Next to bypass the introductory page. The *Select Role Services* page appears.

7. Select the Terminal Server role service, and click Next. The *Uninstall And Reinstall Applications For Compatibility* page appears.

8. Click Next to continue. The *Specify Authentication Method For Terminal Server* page appears.

9. Select the Do Not Require Network Level Authentication option, and click Next. The *Specify Licensing Mode* page appears.

10. Select the Configure Later option, and click Next. The *Select User Groups Allowed To Access This Terminal Server* page appears.

11. Click Add. The Select Users, Computers, Or Groups dialog box appears.

12. In the Enter Object Names To Select box, key **Students**, and click OK.

13. Click Next to accept the specified groups. The *Confirm Installation Selections* page appears.

14. Click Install. The wizard installs the role.

15. Click Close. An Add Roles Wizard message box appears, prompting you to restart the computer.

16. Click Yes. The computer restarts.

17. When the logon screen appears, log on using your *Student##* account and the password *P@ssw0rd*. Server Manager loads and completes the role installation.

18. Click Close.

19. Close Server Manager, and leave the computer logged on for the next exercise.

Exercise 9.2	Configuring RemoteApp Applications
Overview	In this exercise, configure your terminal server to deploy individual applications using RemoteApp.
Completion time	10 minutes

1. Click Start, and then click Administrative Tools > Terminal Services > TS RemoteApp Manager. Click Continue on the User Account Control message box, and the TS RemoteApp Manager console appears, as shown in Figure 9-1.

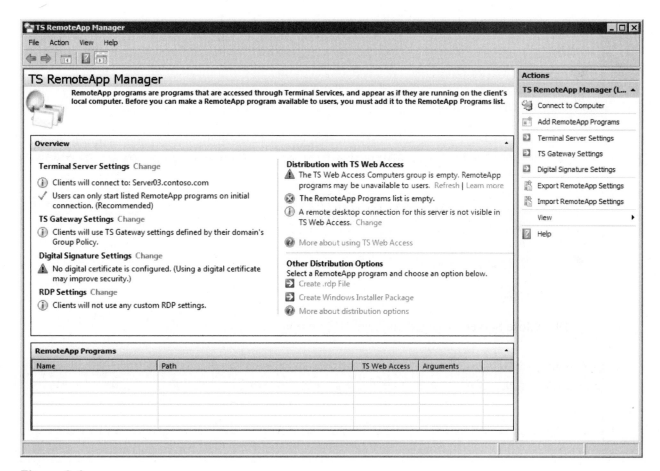

Figure 9-1
TS RemoteApp Manager console

2. In the actions pane, click Add RemoteApp Programs. The RemoteApp Wizard appears.

3. Click Next to bypass the *Welcome* page. The *Choose Programs To Add To The Remoteapp Programs List* page appears.

4. Select the WordPad checkbox, and click Properties. The RemoteApp Properties sheet for WordPad appears.

5. Clear the RemoteApp Program Is Available Through TS Web Access checkbox.

6. Select the Allow Any Command Line Arguments option, and click OK. A RemoteApp Wizard message box appears, warning you that allowing executable files to run with no restrictions on the command-line arguments opens the terminal server to attack.

7. Click Yes.

8. Click Next. The *Review Settings* page appears.

9. Click Finish. The WordPad application appears in the RemoteApp Programs list.

10. Repeat steps 2–9 to add the Server Manager and System Information applications to the RemoteApp Programs list. Clear the RemoteApp Program Is Available Through TS Web Access checkbox, and leave the default Do Not Allow Command-Line Arguments setting for each application.

11. Press Ctrl+Prt Scr to take a screen shot of the TS RemoteApp Manager console showing the applications you added. Press Ctrl+V to paste the image on the page provided in the lab09_worksheet file.

Question 1	In the TS RemoteApp Manager console, three warning indicators are displayed in the Overview area. Will any of these warnings make it impossible to access your RemoteApp applications from your partner server? Explain why or why not.

12. Leave the computer logged on for the next exercise.

Exercise 9.3	Creating RemoteApp RDP Files
Overview	In this exercise, create RDP files that enable clients to access the RemoteApp applications you configured in Exercise 9.2.
Completion time	10 minutes

1. Open the TS RemoteApp Manager console and, in the RemoteApp Programs list, select the WordPad application you added in Exercise 9.2.

2. In the actions pane, select Create .rdp File. The RemoteApp Wizard appears.

3. Click Next to bypass the *Welcome To The RemoteApp Wizard* page. The *Specify Package Settings* page appears, as shown in Figure 9-2.

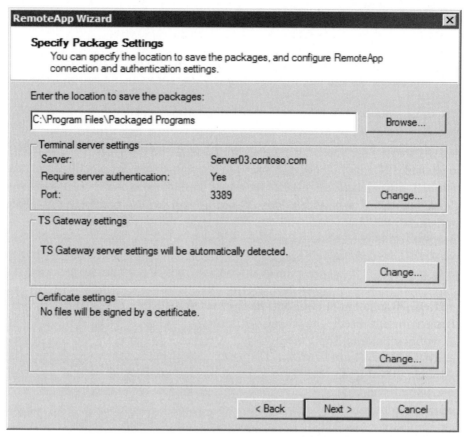

Figure 9-2
Specify Package Settings page of the RemoteApp Wizard

4. In the Enter The Location To Save The Packages text box, key **\\serverdc\students\student##\Documents**, where ## is the number assigned to your computer, and then click Next. The *Review Settings* page appears.

5. Click Finish. The wizard closes, and an RDP file named for the application appears in your Documents folder.

6. Repeat steps 2–5 to create an RDP file for the System Information application in the Documents folder, and then close the TS RemoteApp Manager console.

7. Move to your partner server, and log on using your *Student##* account, where ## is the number assigned to your computer, and the password *P@ssw0rd*.

8.   Open Windows Explorer. The contents of your Documents folder appear.

Question 2	Why is your Documents folder accessible from your partner server?

9.   In the Documents folder, double-click the WordPad RDP file. A RemoteApp message box appears, warning that the publisher of the remote connection cannot be identified.

10. Click Connect. A Windows Security dialog box appears.

11. Authenticate using your *Student##* account and the password *P@ssw0rd*, and click OK. A WordPad window appears.

Question 3	Which computer is running the Wordpad.exe file? How can you tell?

12. In the WordPad window, click File > Open. The Open combo box appears.

13. Browse to the Local Disk (C:) drive.

Question 4	Are you looking at the Local Disk (C:) drive on your partner server or on your computer, the terminal server? How can you tell?

14. Click Cancel to close the Open combo box.

15. While still on your partner server, switch to your Documents folder, and double-click the Msinfo32 RDP file for the System Information application.

16. Click Connect to bypass the Unknown Publisher warning. The System Information window appears.

Question 5	For which computer does the System Information window contain information?

17. Leave the remote application windows open on your partner server, and return to your computer for the next exercise.

Exercise 9.4	Monitoring Terminal Services Activity
Overview	In this exercise, gather information about the Terminal Services sessions currently in use on your server using the Terminal Services Manager console.
Completion time	10 minutes

1. On your server, log on using your *Student##* account and the password *P@ssw0rd*. Click Start, and then click Administrative Tools > Terminal Services > Terminal Services Manager. Click Continue on the User Account Control message box to display the Terminal Services Manager console shown in Figure 9-3.

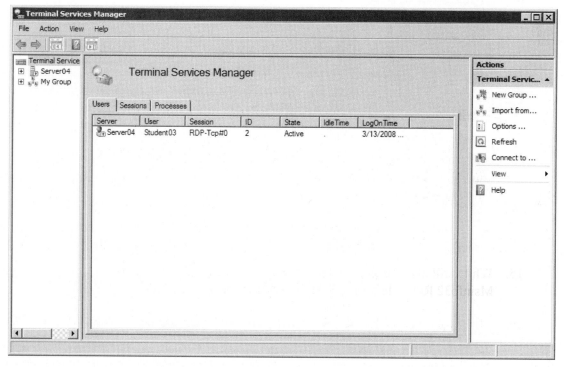

Figure 9-3
Terminal Services Manager console

2. Click the Users tab in the console.

Question 6	How many users are currently connected to the terminal server?

3. Click the Processes tab.

4. Press Ctrl+Prt Scr to take a screen shot of the Terminal Services Manager console showing the Processes tab. Press Ctrl+V to paste the image on the page provided in the lab09_worksheet file.

5. In the Image column, locate the Msinfo32.exe and Wordpad.exe entries. Complete Table 9-1 using the information provided in the console.

Table 9-1

Image	User	Session	ID
Msinfo.exe			
Wordpad.exe			

6. Click the Sessions tab.

Question 7	*How many sessions are listed for the terminal server?*
Question 8	*How can you tell which of the listed sessions correspond to the RemoteApp applications running on your partner server?*

7. Press Ctrl+Prt Scr to take a screen shot of the Terminal Services Manager console showing the Sessions tab. Press Ctrl+V to paste the image on the page provided in the lab09_worksheet file.

8. Select the session corresponding to the RemoteApp applications running on your partner server and, in the actions pane, click Status. A Status window for the session appears.

9. Press Ctrl+Prt Scr to take a screen shot of the Status window. Press Ctrl+V to paste the image on the page provided in the lab09_worksheet file.

10. Click Close.

11. Select the same session again and, in the actions pane, click Disconnect. A Terminal Services Manager message box appears, prompting you to confirm that you want to disconnect the user.

12. Click OK.

Question 9	*What happens in the Terminal Services Manager display?*
Question 10	*What happens on your partner server?*

13. Leave the computer logged on for the next exercise.

Exercise 9.5	Creating RemoteApp MSI Files
Overview	In this exercise, create Microsoft Installer package files that you can use to deploy your RemoteApp applications anywhere on the network.
Completion time	10 minutes

1. Open the TS RemoteApp Manager console and, in the RemoteApp Programs list, select the Server Manager application you added in Exercise 9.2.

2. In the actions pane, select Create Windows Installer Package. The RemoteApp Wizard appears.

3. Click Next to bypass the *Welcome To The RemoteApp Wizard* page. The *Specify Package Settings* page appears.

4. In the Enter The Location To Save The Packages text box, key **serverdc\students\student##\Documents**, where ## is the number assigned to your computer, and then click Next. The *Configure Distribution Package* page appears, as shown in Figure 9-4.

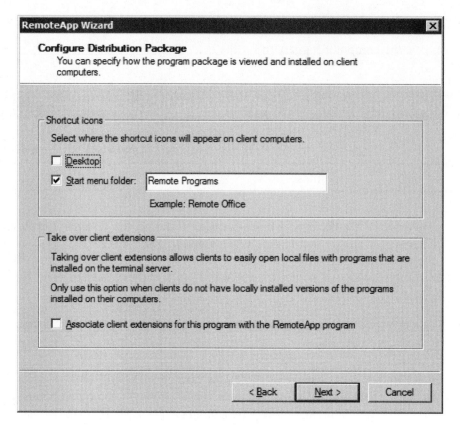

Figure 9-4
Configure Distribution Package page of the RemoteApp Wizard

5. In the Start Menu Folder text box, key **Server## Remote Programs**, where ## is the number assigned to your computer. Then click Next. The *Review Settings* page appears.

6. Click Finish. The wizard closes, and an MSI file named for the application appears in your Documents folder.

7. Move to your partner server, and log on using your *Student##* account, where ## is the number assigned to your computer, and the password *P@ssw0rd*.

8. Open Windows Explorer. The contents of your Documents folder appear.

9. In the Documents folder, double-click the CompMgmtLauncher MSI file. A User Account Control dialog box appears.

10. Click Allow.

11. While still on your partner server, click Start. Then click All Programs > Server## Remote Programs > Server Manager. A RemoteApp message box appears, warning that the remote connection publisher cannot be identified.

12. Click Connect. A Windows Security dialog box appears.

13. Authenticate using your *Student##* account and the password *P@ssw0rd*, and click OK. A Connected To Server##.contoso.com window appears, containing another User Account Control dialog box.

14. Press Ctrl+Prt Scr to take a screen shot of the Connected To Server##.contoso.com window. Press Ctrl+V to paste the image on the page provided in the lab09_worksheet file.

15. In the User Account Control dialog box, click Continue. The Server Manager console appears.

Question 11	Why did two User Account Control dialog boxes appear during the terminal server connection sequence?

16. Return to your server, log on using your *Student##* account and the password *P@ssw0rd*, disconnect all terminal server sessions, close all open windows, and log off of the computer.

LAB REVIEW QUESTIONS

Completion time	5 minutes

1. In Exercise 9.2, if you digitally signed your RemoteApp applications using a digital certificate self-signed by your server, would it enable your partner server to access those applications more securely?

2. In Exercise 9.3, an Unknown Publisher message box appears on your partner server when you execute the WordPad RDP file you created. How can you identify the publisher of the connection and prevent this message box from appearing?

3. In Exercise 9.3, you open two separate RemoteApp applications on your computer, using your partner server as the client. How many sessions did you open on the terminal server by launching these two applications? How can you tell?

LAB CHALLENGE: DEPLOYING REMOTEAPP APPLICATIONS USING GROUP POLICY

Completion time	15 minutes

Your supervisor wants to use RemoteApp and Group Policy to deploy terminal server applications to users' desktops without any configuration by the user. To complete this challenge, demonstrate that this is possible by deploying the Calculator program on your terminal server to all of the other computers on the classroom network. As you proceed, observe the following restrictions.

- Make sure your deployed application is properly identified on the users' desktops as Server## Calculator, where ## is the number assigned to your computer.

- Do not modify any of the existing GPOs in the Active Directory tree. Create a GPO, name it Student##, and link it as needed.

On your worksheet, list all of the tasks you must perform to complete this challenge.

WORKSTATION RESET: RETURN TO BASELINE

Completion time	10 minutes

To accommodate the various classroom configurations supported by this manual, each lab concludes with the student computer returned to the baseline state noted at the end of Exercise 1.1 in Lab 1, "Preparing an Application Server." To return the computer to this state, complete the following procedures.

1. Open the Group Policy Management console, and unlink any GPOs you created during this lab.

2. Open the Server Manager console, and remove the Terminal Services role, as well as any features you added during this lab.

> **NOTE** *Depending on the configuration of your classroom network, it might not be necessary to complete the workstation reset. Check with your instructor before you complete this procedure.*

LAB 10
USING TERMINAL SERVICES WEB ACCESS

This lab contains the following exercises and activities:

Exercise 10.1	Installing the Terminal Services Role
Exercise 10.2	Installing the TS Web Access Role Service
Exercise 10.3	Using Remote Desktop Web Connection
Exercise 10.4	Connecting to a TS Web Access Server
Exercise 10.5	Using RemoteApp with TS Web Access
Lab Review	Questions
Lab Challenge	Using Terminal Services Gateway
Workstation Reset	Return to Baseline

BEFORE YOU BEGIN

The classroom network consists of Windows Server 2008 student servers and the ServerDC connected to a local area network. ServerDC, the domain controller for the contoso.com domain, is running Windows Server 2008. Throughout the labs in this manual, you will install, configure, maintain, and troubleshoot application roles, features, and services on the same student server.

To accommodate various types of classroom arrangements, each lab in this manual assumes that the student servers are in their baseline configuration, as described in Lab 1, "Preparing an

Application Server." If you have not done so already, complete the initial configuration tasks in Exercise 1.1 of Lab 1 before beginning this lab.

Your instructor should have supplied the information needed to complete the following table:

Student computer name (Server##)	
Student account name (Student##)	

To complete the exercises in this lab, you must access a second student computer on the classroom network, referred to in the exercises as your *partner server*. Depending on the network configuration, use one of the following options, as directed by your instructor:

- For a conventional classroom network with one operating system installed on each computer, your lab partner must perform the same exercises on his or her computer, known as your partner server.

- For a classroom in which each computer uses local virtualization software to install multiple operating systems, you must perform the exercises separately on two virtual machines representing your student server and your partner server.

- For a classroom using online virtualization, you must perform the exercises separately on two virtual student servers, representing your student server and your partner server, in your Web browser.

Working with Lab Worksheets

Each lab in this manual requires that you answer questions, save images of your screen, or perform other activities that you document in a worksheet named for the lab, such as *lab10_worksheet*. Your instructor placed the worksheet files in the Students\Worksheets share on ServerDC. As you perform the exercises in each lab, open the appropriate worksheet file using WordPad, fill in the required information, and save the file to your computer's Student##\Documents folder. This folder is automatically redirected to the ServerDC computer. Your instructor will examine these worksheet files to assess your performance.

Use the following procedure to open and save a worksheet file.

1. Click Start, and then click Run. The Run dialog box appears.

2. In the Open text box, key **\\ServerDC\Students\Worksheets\lab##_worksheet** (where lab## contains the number of the lab you're completing), and click OK. The worksheet document opens in WordPad.

3. Complete all of the exercises in the worksheet.

4. In WordPad, choose Save As from the File menu. The Save As dialog box appears.

5. In the File Name text box, key **lab##_worksheet_*yourname*** (where lab## contains the number of the lab you're completing, and *yourname* is your last name), and click Save.

SCENARIO

You are a new administrator for Contoso, Ltd., working on a test deployment of the application server technologies included with Windows Server 2008. In this lab, you explore the Web access capabilities built into Windows Server 2008 Terminal Services.

After completing this lab, you will be able to:

■ Install the TS Web Access role service

■ Configure TS Web Access to deploy Remote Desktop connections and RemoteApp applications

■ Install and configure the TS Gateway role service

Estimated lab time: 80 minutes

Exercise 10.1	Installing the Terminal Services Role
Overview	For Windows Server 2008 to function as a terminal server, you must install the Terminal Services role. If you have not done so already or you are working with a clean virtual machine installation, you must add the role with the Terminal Server role service.
Completion time	10 minutes

1. Turn on your computer. When the logon screen appears, log on using your *Student##* account and the password *P@ssw0rd*.

2. Close the Initial Configuration Tasks window.

3. Open Server Manager, and start the Add Roles Wizard.

4. Click Next to bypass the *Before You Begin* page. The *Select Server Roles* page appears.

> NOTE
>
> *If your computer already has the Terminal Services role installed with its default selection of role services, you can proceed immediately to Exercise 10.2.*

5. Select the Terminal Services checkbox, and click Next. The *Introduction To Terminal Services* page appears.

6. Click Next to bypass the introductory page. The *Select Role Services* page appears.

7. Select the Terminal Server role service, and click Next. The *Uninstall And Reinstall Applications For Compatibility* page appears.

8. Click Next to continue. The *Specify Authentication Method For Terminal Server* page appears.

9. Select the Do Not Require Network Level Authentication option, and click Next. The *Specify Licensing Mode* page appears.

10. Select the Configure Later option, and click Next. The *Select User Groups Allowed To Access This Terminal Server* page appears.

11. Click Add. The Select Users, Computers, Or Groups dialog box appears.

12. In the Enter Object Names To Select box, key **Students**, and click OK.

13. Click Next to accept the specified groups. The *Confirm Installation Selections* page appears.

14. Click Install. The wizard installs the role.

15. Click Close. The Add Roles Wizard message box appears, prompting you to restart the computer.

16. Click Yes. The computer restarts.

17. When the logon screen appears, log on using your *Student##* account and the password *P@ssw0rd*. Server Manager loads and completes the role installation.

18. Click Close.

Exercise 10.2 Installing the TS Web Access Role Service

Overview	In this exercise, add the TS Web Access role service to the Terminal Services configuration. This enables users to connect to the terminal server using Internet Explorer instead of the Remote Desktop Connection client.
Completion time	5 minutes

1. In Server Manager, select the Roles node and, under Terminal Services, click Add Role Services. The *Select Role Services* page appears, as shown in Figure 10-1.

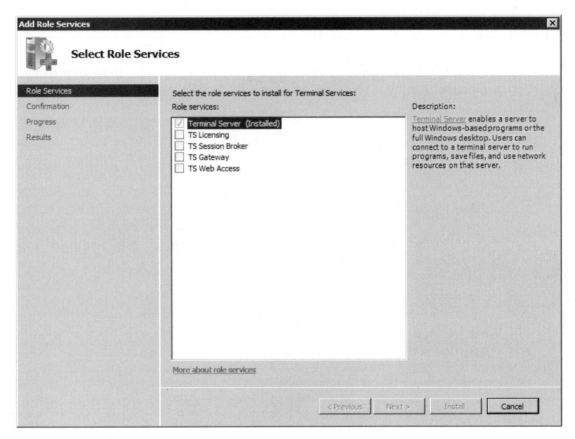

Figure 10-1
Select Role Services page in the Add Role Services Wizard

2. Select the TS Web Access checkbox. The Add Role Services And Features Required For TS Web Access? dialog box appears, prompting you to install the Web Server (IIS) role and the Windows Process Activation Service feature.

3. Click Add Required Role Services, and then click Next three times to accept the default Web Services (IIS) selections. The *Confirm Installation Selections* page appears.

4. Click Install. The wizard installs the role services.

5. Click Close. The wizard closes.

6. Close the Server Manager console.

7. Log off of the computer.

Exercise 10.3	Using Remote Desktop Web Connection
Overview	In this exercise, use the Remote Desktop Web Connection client on your partner server to connect to your own terminal server.
Completion time	15 minutes

1. After you and your partner have completed Exercise 10.2, move to your partner server, and log on using your *Student##* account with the password *P@ssw0rd*.

2. Open Internet Explorer and, in the address box, key **http://server##.contoso.com/ts,** where ## is the number assigned to your server, and press Enter. A Connect To Server##.contoso.com dialog box appears.

3. Log on using your *Student##* account and the password *P@ssw0rd*. An Internet Explorer window appears that contains the *TS Web Access* page with an information bar at the top, as shown in Figure 10-2, warning you that the Web site wants to install an ActiveX control. An Information Bar message box also appears, alerting you to the information bar's presence.

Figure 10-2
TS Web Access page in Internet Explorer

4. In the Information Bar message box, select the Don't Show This Message Again checkbox, and click Close. The message box disappears.

5. In the Internet Explorer window, click the information bar and, on the context menu, select Run ActiveX Control. An Internet Explorer – Security Warning message box appears.

6. Click Run to install the ActiveX control. The *TS Web Access* page reloads.

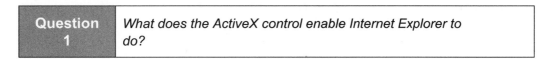

Question 1	*What does the ActiveX control enable Internet Explorer to do?*

7. Click Remote Desktop. The *Terminal Services Remote Desktop Web Connection* page appears with another information bar.

8. Click the information bar, and install this ActiveX control as you installed the previous one.

9. Press Ctrl+Prt Scr to take a screen shot of the Internet Explorer window showing the *Terminal Services Remote Desktop Web Connection* page. Press Ctrl+V to paste the image on the page provided in the lab10_worksheet file.

10. In the Connect To text box, key **server##.contoso.com**, where ## is the number of your terminal server.

11. In the Remote Desktop Size drop-down list, select 800 x 600 Pixels.

12. Click the Options button. Additional checkboxes and drop-down lists appear on the page.

13. In the Remote Computer Sound drop-down list, select Do Not Play.

14. In the Performance drop-down list, select LAN (10 Mbps or higher).

15. Click Connect. A Remote Desktop Connection dialog box appears, warning you that the publisher of the remote connection is unknown.

16. Click Connect. A Windows Security dialog box appears.

17. Log on using your *Student##* account and the password *P@ssw0rd*. A Remote Desktop window appears containing a Terminal Services session.

18. In the Remote Desktop session window, click Start, and log off of the session. The Remote Desktop window closes.

19. Log off of your partner server.

Exercise 10.4	Connecting to a TS Web Access Server
Overview	In this exercise, configure your terminal server to deploy a Remote Desktop client to Internet Explorer on your partner server.
Completion time	10 minutes

1. On your own server, log on using your *Student##* account and the password *P@ssw0rd*.

2. Open the TS RemoteApp Manager console.

3. In the actions pane, click Terminal Server Settings. The RemoteApp Deployment Settings dialog box appears, as shown in Figure 10-3.

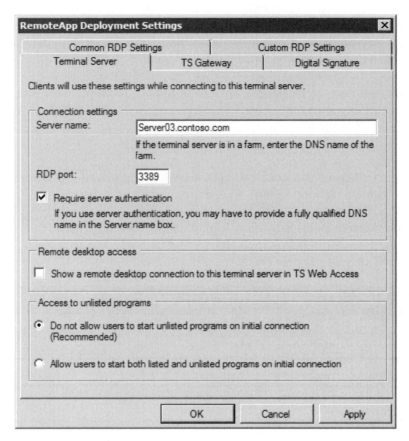

Figure 10-3
RemoteApp Deployment Settings dialog box

4.   In the Remote Desktop Access box, select the Show A Remote Desktop Connection To This Terminal Server In TS Web Access checkbox.

5.   Click OK.

6.   Close the TS RemoteApp Manager console.

7.   Return to your partner server, and log on using your *Student##* account and the password *P@ssw0rd*.

8.   Open Internet Explorer, and connect again to server##.contoso.com/ts, where ## is the number of your terminal server.

Question 2	What change occurred in the TS Web Access page because you selected the Show A Remote Desktop Connection To This Terminal Server In TS Web Access checkbox?

9. Press Ctrl+Prt Scr to take a screen shot of the Internet Explorer window showing the *TS Web Access* page. Press Ctrl+V to paste the image on the page provided in the lab10_worksheet file.

10. Click the Remote Desktop icon. The Remote Desktop Connection dialog box appears, citing an unknown publisher.

11. Click Connect.

12. Log on using your *Student##* account and the password *P@ssw0rd*, and then click OK. The Remote Desktop session appears.

13. In the Remote Desktop session, log off of the terminal server.

14. Log off of your partner server.

Exercise 10.5	Using RemoteApp with TS Web Access
Overview	In this exercise, configure your terminal server to deploy RemoteApp applications using TS Web Access.
Completion time	10 minutes

1. On your own server, log on using your *Student##* account and the password *P@ssw0rd*.

2. Open the TS RemoteApp Manager console.

> **NOTE**
> *If your computer already has RemoteApp applications installed from Lab 9, open the Properties sheet for each one, and select the RemoteApp Program Is Available Through TS Web Access checkbox. You can then proceed immediately to Step 7.*

3. In the actions pane, click Add RemoteApp Programs. The RemoteApp Wizard appears.

4. Click Next to bypass the *Welcome* page. The *Choose Programs To Add To The Remoteapp Programs List* page appears.

5. Select the following checkboxes, and click Next. The *Review Settings* page appears.

   - Server Manager

   - System Information

   - WordPad

6. Click Finish. The applications appear in the RemoteApp Programs list.

7. Log off of your server, and move to your partner server, logging on using your *Student##* account and the password *P@ssw0rd*.

8. Open Internet Explorer, and connect again to server##.contoso.com, where ## is the number of your terminal server.

Question 3	What is different about the TS Web Access page when compared with the display you saw in the previous exercise?

9. Press Ctrl+Prt Scr to take a screen shot of the Internet Explorer window. Press Ctrl+V to paste the image on the page provided in the lab10_worksheet file.

10. Click the WordPad icon.

11. Click Connect to bypass the Unknown Publisher warning dialog box.

12. Log on to the terminal server using your *Student##* account and the password *P@ssw0rd*. A WordPad window appears on the desktop.

13. Click Start, and then click All Programs > Accessories > WordPad. A second WordPad window appears on the desktop.

Question 4	Can you detect any difference between the two WordPad windows?

14. Close all open windows, and log off of your partner server.

LAB REVIEW QUESTIONS

Completion time   5 minutes

1. The IIS7 Web site you connected to initially in Exercise 10.3 uses HTTP for its client/server communications. Your Terminal Services session uses RDP. At what point during the connection process does the client computer switch from using HTTP to RDP for its communications with the terminal server?

2. How does connecting to the terminal server with the Remote Desktop icon, as you did in Exercise 10.4, differ from the Terminal Services Remote Desktop Web Connection you used in Exercise 10.3?

LAB CHALLENGE: USING TERMINAL SERVICES GATEWAY

Completion time	25 minutes

Your supervisor wants you to demonstrate how the TS Gateway role service can enable RDC clients on the Internet to access the company's terminal servers securely. To complete this challenge, you must install and configure the TS Gateway role service on your server so that it can provide access to Terminal Services on your partner server. Then, you must configure Remote Desktop Connection to use the TS Gateway service on your partner server so that you can access Terminal Services on your own server. When the configuration is complete, your server and your partner server should be able to communicate as shown in Figure 10-4.

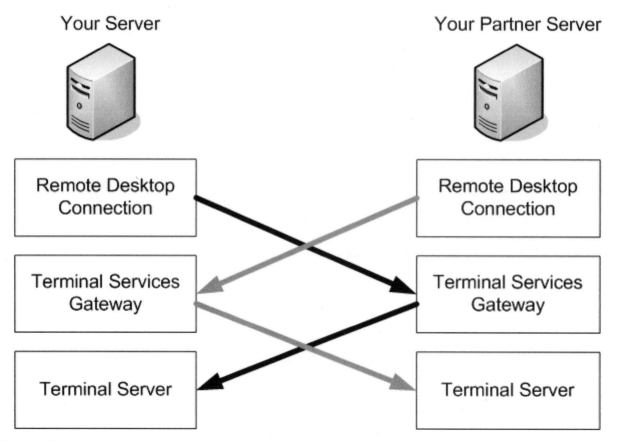

Figure 10-4
Terminal Services Gateway communications

List the tasks you must complete to install and configure the Terminal Services components, and then take a screen shot of the TS Gateway Manager console showing the connected client. Paste the image on the page provided in the lab10_worksheet file.

WORKSTATION RESET: RETURN TO BASELINE

Completion time	10 minutes

After this lab, you will not need the Terminal Services or Web Server (IIS) roles installed on your server until Lab 12. To return the computer to its baseline state, complete the following procedures.

1. Open the Server Manager console. Remove the Terminal Services role and Web Server (IIS) role, as well as any features you added during this lab.

LAB 11
USING NETWORK APPLICATION SERVICES

This lab contains the following exercises and activities:

BEFORE YOU BEGIN

The classroom network consists of Windows Server 2008 student servers and the ServerDC connected to a local area network. ServerDC, the domain controller for the contoso.com domain, is running Windows Server 2008. Throughout the labs in this manual, you will install, configure, maintain, and troubleshoot application roles, features, and services on the same student server.

To accommodate various types of classroom arrangements, each lab in this manual assumes that the student servers are in their baseline configuration, as described in Lab 1, "Preparing an Application Server." If you have not done so already, complete the initial configuration tasks in Exercise 1.1 of Lab 1 before beginning this lab.

Your instructor should have supplied the information needed to complete the following table:

Student computer name (Server##)	
Student account name (Student##)	

Working with Lab Worksheets

Each lab in this manual requires that you answer questions, save images of your screen, or perform other activities that you document in a worksheet named for the lab, such as *lab11_worksheet*. Your instructor placed the worksheet files in the Students\Worksheets share on ServerDC. As you perform the exercises in each lab, open the appropriate worksheet file using WordPad, fill in the required information, and save the file to your computer's Student##\Documents folder. This folder is automatically redirected to the ServerDC computer. Your instructor will examine these worksheet files to assess your performance.

Use the following procedure to open and save a worksheet file.

1. Click Start, and then click Run. The Run dialog box appears.

2. In the Open text box, key **\\ServerDC\Students\Worksheets\lab##_worksheet** (where lab## contains the number of the lab you're completing), and click OK. The worksheet document opens in WordPad.

3. Complete all of the exercises in the worksheet.

4. In WordPad, choose Save As from the File menu. The Save As dialog box appears.

5. In the File Name text box, key **lab##_worksheet_*yourname*** (where lab## contains the number of the lab you're completing, and *yourname* is your last name), and click Save.

SCENARIO

You are a new administrator for Contoso, Ltd., working on a test deployment of the application server technologies included with Windows Server 2008. In this lab, you explore some of the add-on network applications that Microsoft provides for Windows Server 2008.

After completing this lab, you will be able to:

- Install and configure the Streaming Media Services role

- Install, configure, and use Windows SharePoint Services

Estimated lab time: 95 minutes

Exercise 11.1	Installing Windows Media Services
Overview	Windows Server 2008 does not ship with the Streaming Media Services role; it is a separate download. Your instructor has placed the software add-on on the classroom server. In this exercise, install the Windows Media Services software, which makes the Streaming Media Services role appear in Server Manager.
Completion time	10 minutes

1. Turn on your computer. When the logon screen appears, log on using your *Student##* account and the password *P@ssw0rd*.

2. Close the Initial Configuration Tasks window.

3. Open Windows Explorer, and browse to the \\ServerDC\Install\MediaSvcs folder.

4. Double-click the Windows6.0-KB934518-x86-Server.msu file. Click Continue in the User Account Control message box. The Windows Update Standalone Installer message box appears, confirming that you want to install the update.

5. Click OK. The Read These License Terms window appears.

6. Click I Accept to agree to the terms. The *Download And Install Updates* page appears.

7. When the *Installation Complete* page appears, click Close.

8. Open Server Manager, and start the Add Roles Wizard.

Question 1	*What change in Server Manager was caused by the Windows Media Services installation you just performed?*

9. On the *Select Server Roles* page, select Streaming Media Services, and click Next.

10. Click Next again to bypass the introductory page. The *Select Role Services* page appears, as shown in Figure 11-1.

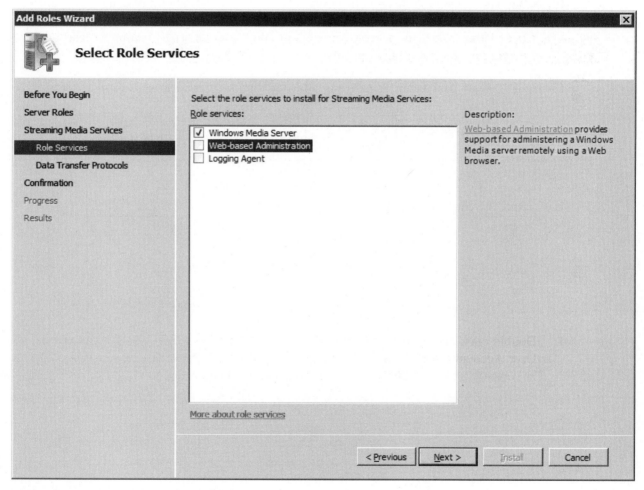

Figure 11-1
Select Role Services page in the Add Role Services Wizard

11. Select Web-Based Administration. An Add Role Services And Features Required For Web-Based Administration dialog box appears.

12. Click Add Required Role Services, and then click Next. The *Select Data Transfer Protocols* page appears.

Question 2	*Why is the Hypertext Transfer Protocol (HTTP) option unavailable (gray) in the Select Data Transfer Protocols page?*

13. Click Next to accept the default settings. The *Web Server (IIS)* introductory page appears.

14. Click Next twice to accept the default Web Server (IIS) settings. The *Confirm Installation Selections* page appears.

15. Click Install. The wizard installs the role, and the *Installation Results* page appears.

16. Press Ctrl+Prt Scr to take a screen shot of the *Installation Results* page. Press Ctrl+V to paste the image on the page provided in the lab11_worksheet file.

17. Click Close.

18. Leave the computer logged on for the next exercise.

Exercise 11.2	Creating a Publishing Point
Overview	In this exercise, create a new publishing point that you can use to deploy multimedia content to network clients on your Windows Media Services server.
Completion time	10 minutes

1. Click Start, and then click Administrative Tools > Windows Media Services. Click Continue in the User Account Control message box. The Windows Media Services console appears, as shown in Figure 11-2.

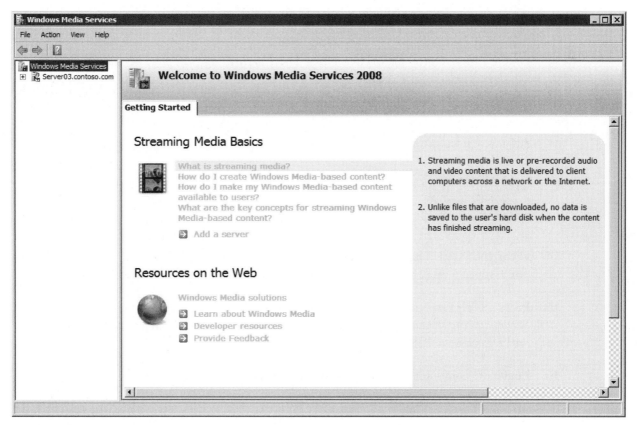

Figure 11-2
Windows Media Services console

2. In the scope (left) pane, expand your server, and select the Publishing Points node. The *Publishing Points On Server##.contoso.com* page appears.

3. Right-click the Publishing Points node and, from the context menu, select Add Publishing Point (Wizard). The Add Publishing Point Wizard appears.

4.   Click Next to bypass the *Welcome* page. The *Publishing Point Name* page appears.

5.   In the Name text box, key **Stream##**, where ## is the number assigned to your computer, and click Next. The *Content Type* page appears.

6.   Select the One File option, and click Next. The *Publishing Point Type* page appears.

7.   Select the On-Demand Publishing Point option, and click Next. The *Existing Publishing Point* page appears.

8.   Leave the Add A New Publishing Point option selected, and click Next. The *File Location* page appears.

9.   Click Browse. The Windows Media Browse dialog box appears.

10. Select the Industrial.wmv media file, and click Select File.

11. On the *File Location* page, click Next. The *Unicast Logging* page appears.

12. Select the Yes, Enable Logging For This Publishing Point checkbox, and click Next. The *Publishing Point Summary* page appears.

13. Click Next. The *Completing The Add Publishing Point Wizard* page appears.

Question 3	*What URL must clients use to access the publishing point you just created?*

14. Clear the After The Wizard Finishes checkbox, and click Finish. The new publishing point appears on the *Publishing Points On Server##.contoso.com* page.

15. Press Ctrl+Prt Scr to take a screen shot of the *Publishing Points On Server##.contoso.com* page. Press Ctrl+V to paste the image on the page provided in the lab11_worksheet file.

16. Leave the computer logged on for the next exercise.

Exercise 11.3	Creating an Announcement File
Overview	In this exercise, create an announcement file and a Web page that clients can use to access multimedia content on the publishing point you created in Exercise 11.2.
Completion time	5 minutes

1. In the Windows Media Services console, expand the Publishing Points node, and select the Stream## publishing point you just created, as shown in Figure 11-3.

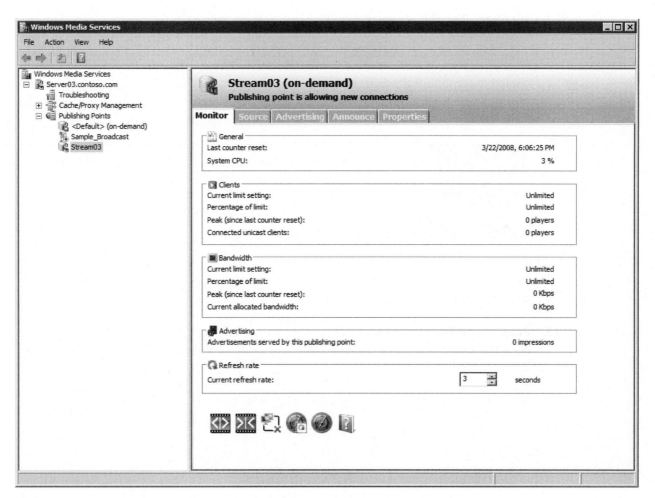

Figure 11-3
Monitor tab of a Windows Media Services publishing point

2. In the detail pane, click the Announce tab.

3. Click the Run Unicast Announcement Wizard button. The *Welcome To The Unicast Announcement Wizard* page appears.

4. Click Next. The *Access The Content* page appears.

5. Click Next to accept the default URL. The *Save Announcement Options* page appears.

6. Select the Create A Web Page With An Embedded Player And A Link To The Content checkbox.

7. Press Ctrl+Prt Scr to take a screen shot of the *Save Announcement Options* page. Press Ctrl+V to paste the image on the page provided in the lab11_worksheet file.

8. Click Next. The *Edit Announcement Metadata* page appears.

9. Click Next to accept the default values. The *Completing The Unicast Announcement Wizard* page appears.

10. Clear the Test Files When This Wizard Finishes checkbox, and click Finish. The wizard creates the announcement file and a Web page containing the embedded player.

Question 4	*Does the announcement file the wizard created contain the actual multimedia content? How can you tell?*

11. Leave the computer logged on for the next exercise.

Exercise 11.4	Establishing a Windows Media Services Connection
Overview	In this exercise, test your Windows Media Services server by using the Web page you created to access your new publishing point.
Completion time	10 minutes

1. Open Internet Explorer. In the address box, key **http://server##.contoso.com/stream##.htm**, and then press Enter. The *Announcement For Publishing Point Stream##* page appears, as shown in Figure 11-4.

> **NOTE**
>
> *If an information bar appears in the Internet Explorer window warning you about the potential dangers of ActiveX content, click the bar and allow IE to run the ActiveX control.*

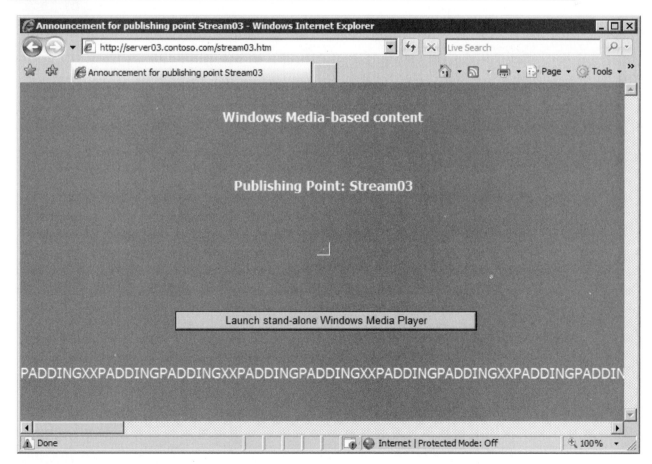

Figure 11-4
Announcement For Publishing Point Stream## page

Question 5	What happens after the Announcement For Publishing Point Stream## page appears?

2. Click the Launch Stand-Alone Windows Media Player button.

Question 6	What happens?

3. Open the Server Manager console, and start the Add Features Wizard.

4. On the *Select Features* page, select the Desktop Experience feature, and click Next.

5. Click Install. The wizard installs the selected feature.

6. Click Close, and restart the computer.

7. After the computer starts, Server Manager reloads itself and completes the feature installation.

8. Click Close.

9. Open Internet Explorer and try again to connect to the URL http://server##.contoso.com/stream##.htm.

Question 7	What is the result?

10. Press Ctrl+Prt Scr to take a screen shot of the *Announcement For Publishing Point Stream##* page showing the embedded multimedia content. Press Ctrl+V to paste the image on the page provided in the lab11_worksheet file.

11. Close all open windows, and log off of your computer.

LAB REVIEW QUESTIONS

Completion time	5 minutes

1. When a client computer accesses multimedia content by executing an announcement file on a media server, should Windows Media Player be installed on the client or the server?

2. In its default state, immediately after installation, is Windows Media Services ready to stream multimedia content to clients? Why or why not?

3. In Exercise 11.4, why does the multimedia file not play the first time you access the *Announcement For Publishing Point Stream##* page in Internet Explorer?

LAB CHALLENGE: DEPLOYING WINDOWS SHAREPOINT SERVICES

Completion time	40 minutes

The director of the IT department is considering a large deployment of Windows SharePoint Services to enable network users to share documents and collaborate on projects at the workgroup and departmental levels. To help her decide, she wants you to deploy Windows SharePoint Services on a Windows Server 2008 test server by completing each of the following tasks:

- Install and configure Windows SharePoint Services.

- Add the Students group as SharePoint team site users, giving them the Contribute permission.

- Add a new shared document to the Team Site library.

- Add a calendar entry scheduling a staff meeting.

> **NOTE**
> *Windows SharePoint Services is not supplied with Windows Server 2008. It is available as a free download from Microsoft's Web site. However, your instructor placed the software on the network server in the \\ServerDC\Install\SharePoint folder.*

List the steps you must perform to complete these tasks, and take screen shots demonstrating that you have completed each task. Paste the images on the page provided in the lab11_worksheet file.

WORKSTATION RESET: RETURN TO BASELINE

Completion time	15 minutes

After this lab, you will not need the Windows Media Services role or the Windows SharePoint Services application. To return the computer to its baseline state, complete the following procedures.

1. Open the Server Manager console, and remove all of the roles you installed during this lab. Restart the computer.

2. Open the Server Manager console, and remove all of the features you installed during this lab. Restart the computer.

3. Open the Programs And Features control panel, and uninstall Microsoft Windows SharePoint Services 3.0. Restart the computer.

LAB 12
CLUSTERING SERVERS

This lab contains the following exercises and activities:

Lab Challenge 1   Creating a Terminal Services Server Farm

Lab Challenge 2   Creating a Failover Cluster

Lab Review   Questions

BEFORE YOU BEGIN

The classroom network consists of Windows Server 2008 student servers and the ServerDC connected to a local area network. ServerDC, the domain controller for the contoso.com domain, is running Windows Server 2008. Throughout the labs in this manual, you will install, configure, maintain, and troubleshoot application roles, features, and services on the same student server.

To accommodate various types of classroom arrangements, each lab in this manual assumes that the student servers are in their baseline configuration, as described in Lab 1, "Preparing an Application Server." If you have not done so already, complete the initial configuration tasks in Exercise 1.1 of Lab 1 before beginning this lab.

Your instructor should have supplied the information needed to complete the following table:

Student computer name (Server##)	
Student account name (Student##)	

To complete the exercises in this lab, you must access a second student computer on the classroom network, referred to in the exercises as your *partner server*. Depending on the network configuration, use one of the following options, as directed by your instructor:

- For a conventional classroom network with one operating system installed on each computer, your lab partner must perform the same exercises on his or her computer, known as your partner server.

- For a classroom in which each computer uses local virtualization software to install multiple operating systems, you must perform the exercises separately on two virtual machines representing your student server and your partner server.

- For a classroom using online virtualization, you must perform the exercises separately on two virtual student servers, representing your student server and your partner server, in your Web browser.

For this lab, each pair of partner servers must work more cooperatively than they have before. Instead of each server performing the same exercises and then using the partner server as a test client, this lab requires that you create two types of server clusters, in which the computers are joined to run the same application.

Working with Lab Worksheets

Each lab in this manual requires that you answer questions, save images of your screen, or perform other activities that you document in a worksheet named for the lab, such as *lab12_worksheet*. Your instructor placed the worksheet files in the Students\Worksheets share on ServerDC. As you perform the exercises in each lab, open the appropriate worksheet file using WordPad, fill in the required information, and save the file to your computer's Student##\Documents folder. This folder is automatically redirected to the ServerDC computer. Your instructor will examine these worksheet files to assess your performance.

Use the following procedure to open and save a worksheet file.

1. Click Start, and then click Run. The Run dialog box appears.

2. In the Open text box, key **ServerDC\Students\Worksheets\lab##_worksheet** (where lab## contains the number of the lab you're completing), and click OK. The worksheet document opens in WordPad.

3. Complete all of the exercises in the worksheet.

4. In WordPad, choose Save As from the File menu. The Save As dialog box appears.

5. In the File Name text box, key **lab##_worksheet_*yourname*** (where lab## contains the number of the lab you're completing, and *yourname* is your last name), and click Save.

SCENARIO

You are a new administrator for Contoso, Ltd., working on a test deployment of the application server technologies included with Windows Server 2008. In this lab, you explore some of the high-availability features included with Windows Server 2008.

After completing this lab, you will be able to:

- Install and configure a Terminal Services server farm

- Install and configure a failover cluster

Estimated lab time: 75 minutes

LAB CHALLENGE 1: CREATING A TERMINAL SERVICES SERVER FARM

Completion time	30 minutes

Contoso, Ltd. plans to deploy many new workstations using terminal servers to host applications for them. Because multiple terminal servers are needed, your department is exploring the construction of a Windows Server 2008 terminal server farm, consisting of multiple computers balancing the client load between them.

To complete this challenge, you must install and configure Terminal Services on your server and your partner server to create a terminal server farm called FARM##, where ## is the number assigned to the server running the TS Session Broker role service. Use DNS round robin to balance the incoming traffic load between the two servers.

Connect to the server farm using the Remote Desktop Connection client, and use the Terminal Services Manager console to monitor the activity on the server farm.

Document your procedures by listing all of the tasks you completed during installation and configuration. Take screen shots of the Terminal Services Configuration, Terminal Services Manager, and DNS Manager consoles illustrating all of the completed tasks.

When you are finished, remove all of the roles and features you installed on both computers before you proceed to the next exercise.

LAB CHALLENGE 2: CREATING A FAILOVER CLUSTER

Completion time	45 minutes

After suffering a serious server outage, Contoso, Ltd. decided to implement its business-critical applications using failover clusters. You must create a test deployment of a two-node failover cluster on your lab network. To complete this challenge, install the Failover Clustering feature, and use it to validate, create, and configure a failover cluster using your server and your partner server. Give the failover cluster the name Cluster##, where ## is the number assigned to the server on which you created the cluster.

After you complete the configuration process, demonstrate the cluster's functionality by monitoring the cluster on your server as you move the cluster##other application from one server to the other.

Document your procedures by listing all of the completed installation and configuration tasks. Save the Failover Cluster Validation Report to your Documents folder. Take screen shots of the Failover Cluster Management console illustrating the completed tasks and the cluster's functionality.

LAB REVIEW QUESTIONS

Completion time	5 minutes

1. What is the fundamental difference between a server farm and a failover cluster?

2. In a Terminal Services server farm, why is it necessary to have a second load balancing mechanism, such as DNS round robin, in addition to TS Session Broker?

3. In Lab Challenge 2, you created a failover cluster without a shared storage mechanism. If you were to install a shared storage mechanism on your lab network, what would be the advantages of using iSCSI instead of Fibre Channel?